The UK
Mediterranean Air Fryer
Cookbook for Beginners

Quick and Nutritious Mediterranean Air Fryer Recipes to Take You Through the Richness of Mediterranean Cuisine | Full-Colour Edition

Imogene Wiese

© **Copyright 2024 –All Rights Reserved**

This document is geared towards providing exact and reliable information concerning the topic and issue covered.

In no way is it legal to reproduce, duplicate, or transmit any part of this document in either electronic means or printed format. Recording this publication is strictly prohibited. Any storage of this document is not allowed unless with written permission from the publisher.

All rights reserved. The information provided herein is stated to be truthful and consistent, in that any liability, in terms of inattention or otherwise, by any usage or abuse of any policies, processes, or directions contained within is the solitary and utter responsibility of the recipient reader.

Under no circumstances will any legal responsibility or blame be held against the publisher for any reparation, damages, or monetary loss due to the information herein, either directly or indirectly. Respective authors own all copyrights not held by the publisher.

The information herein is offered for informational purposes solely and is universal as so. The presentation of the information is without a contract or any type of guarantee assurance. The trademarks used are without any consent, and the publication of any trademark is without permission or backing by the trademark owner.

All trademarks and brands within this book are for clarifying purposes only, are owned by the owners themselves, and are not affiliated with this document.

Contents

- 1   Introduction
- 2   Fundamentals of Mediterranean Diet
- 12   4-Week Meal Plan
- 14   Chapter 1 Breakfast
- 22   Chapter 2 Vegetarian Mains
- 30   Chapter 3 Snacks and Sides
- 37   Chapter 4 Pizza, Bread and Pasta
- 43   Chapter 5 Fish and Seafood Mains
- 49   Chapter 6 Poultry Mains
- 55   Chapter 7 Red Meat Mains
- 61   Chapter 8 Sweets and Desserts
- 67   Conclusion
- 68   Appendix Recipes Index

Introduction

Welcome to the Mediterranean Air Fryer Cookbook, your guide to enjoying the fresh, vibrant flavours of the Mediterranean diet with the convenience of an air fryer. Whether you're new to air frying or a seasoned user, this cookbook will help you create delicious, nutritious meals that celebrate the wholesome ingredients and culinary traditions of Mediterranean cuisine.

The Mediterranean diet, renowned for its health benefits, is rich in fruits, vegetables, whole grains, lean proteins, and healthy fats like olive oil. It's a way of eating that's not only delicious but also heart-healthy, helping to reduce the risk of chronic diseases such as heart disease, diabetes, and obesity. This cookbook brings you a variety of traditional Mediterranean dishes, all adapted for the air fryer, making it easier than ever to enjoy these healthful recipes at home.

The air fryer allows you to prepare crispy, flavourful meals with a fraction of the oil typically used in traditional frying methods. From golden falafel and roasted vegetables to succulent chicken and fish, the air fryer's ability to cook food quickly and evenly ensures that each meal is both healthy and satisfying.

Inside, you'll find a wide range of recipes, from appetisers and mains to sides and desserts, each one infused with the rich, sun-kissed flavours of the Mediterranean. Every recipe is designed to be simple to follow, with clear instructions, ensuring success in the kitchen every time.

Whether you're looking to maintain a healthier lifestyle or simply enjoy the incredible flavours of Mediterranean cooking, this cookbook will help you create meals that are as nutritious as they are delicious.

Fundamentals of Mediterranean Diet

The Mediterranean diet is widely regarded as one of the healthiest and most balanced diets in the world, promoting not only physical health but also a positive, sustainable lifestyle. Originating from the countries surrounding the Mediterranean Sea, this diet is based on traditional eating habits that date back centuries. It emphasises fresh, whole foods, moderate consumption, and a lifestyle rich in physical activity, social connections, and a focus on enjoying meals. In this chapter, we will explore the Mediterranean diet in detail, including its definition, origins, dietary structure, key characteristics, important considerations, health benefits, and overall impact.

What is Mediterranean Diet?

The Mediterranean diet is a nutritional pattern inspired by the traditional dietary habits of countries bordering the Mediterranean Sea, including Greece, Italy, Spain, and southern France. It is characterised by an emphasis on plant-based foods, healthy fats, and lean proteins, combined with moderate physical activity and a social, mindful approach to eating. Unlike many modern diets, the Mediterranean diet is not restrictive but rather focuses on balance, encouraging the consumption of natural, whole foods while minimising processed items.

Origins of the Mediterranean Diet

The origins of the Mediterranean diet can be traced back to the mid-20th century when researchers, notably American physiologist Dr Ancel Keys, observed that populations in Mediterranean countries had lower rates of chronic diseases such as heart disease, cancer, and diabetes compared to other parts of the world. Keys conducted the famous "Seven Countries Study," which examined the dietary habits and health outcomes of populations across different regions. His findings revealed that people in Mediterranean regions who followed traditional diets had significantly better heart health and longevity. These results spurred further research into the benefits of the Mediterranean diet, leading to its recognition as one of the healthiest ways to eat.

Structure of the Mediterranean Diet

The Mediterranean diet follows a simple but effective structure, prioritising the consumption of fresh, seasonal ingredients and whole foods. The diet can be broken down into the following components:

- **Fruits and Vegetables:** A wide variety of fresh, seasonal fruits and vegetables form the foundation of the Mediterranean diet. These provide essential vitamins, minerals, fibre, and antioxidants, all of which support overall health.
- **Whole Grains:** Whole grains such as brown rice, quinoa, wholemeal bread, and oats are preferred over refined grains. These are rich in fibre and help regulate blood sugar levels while providing sustained energy.
- **Healthy Fats:** Olive oil is a key ingredient in the Mediterranean diet, often replacing butter and margarine as the primary source of fat. Rich in monounsaturated fats, olive oil supports heart health. Other sources of healthy fats include avocados, nuts, and seeds.
- **Legumes and Pulses:** Beans, lentils, and chickpeas are staples of the diet, providing protein and fibre. These plant-based proteins help to lower cholesterol levels and support digestive health.
- **Lean Proteins:** Fish and seafood, particularly oily fish like salmon, sardines, and mackerel, are consumed regularly due to their omega-3 fatty acids, which protect the heart. Poultry and eggs are eaten in moderation, while red meat is limited.
- **Dairy:** Dairy products such as yoghurt and cheese are consumed in moderation. In the Mediterranean diet, dairy is typically eaten in its fermented form, which supports gut health.
- **Herbs and Spices:** Instead of salt, meals are flavoured with herbs, garlic, and spices, which add flavour without increasing sodium intake.
- **Red Wine:** Moderate consumption of red wine, usually with meals, is part of the Mediterranean lifestyle. Red wine is rich in antioxidants, such as resveratrol, which have been linked to heart health. However, wine consumption is entirely optional and should be limited to no more than one glass per day for women and two for men.
- **Physical Activity:** While not a dietary component, regular physical activity is an essential part of the Mediterranean lifestyle. Walking, cycling, and engaging in social activities help maintain a healthy body weight and promote overall well-being.

Key Characteristics of the Mediterranean Diet

The Mediterranean diet is distinguished by several key characteristics that set it apart from other dietary patterns:

- **Focus on Plant-Based Foods:** Vegetables, fruits, legumes, and whole grains are prioritised in every meal. These foods provide essential nutrients, fibre, and antioxidants that support health and reduce inflammation.
- **High in Healthy Fats:** The diet encourages the consumption of monounsaturated fats, particularly from olive oil,

which has anti-inflammatory properties and helps lower cholesterol.
- **Limited Processed Foods:** Processed foods, sugars, and refined grains are minimised in favour of fresh, whole ingredients.
- **Moderate Protein Consumption:** The Mediterranean diet focuses on lean proteins such as fish and poultry, while red meat is consumed sparingly.
- **Mindful Eating and Social Meals:** Eating is considered a social and mindful activity. Meals are often shared with family and friends, promoting connection and relaxation, which can aid digestion.
- **Moderation in All Things:** The Mediterranean diet promotes a balanced, moderate approach to eating and drinking. Portion control and mindful consumption are emphasised, without the need for calorie counting.

Benefits of Mediterranean Diet

The Mediterranean diet is widely recognised for its numerous health benefits. Research has consistently shown that following this diet can help reduce the risk of chronic diseases and improve overall well-being. Key health benefits include:

- **Heart Health:** The Mediterranean diet is associated with a lower risk of cardiovascular diseases, including heart attacks, strokes, and hypertension. The diet's emphasis on healthy fats, such as those found in olive oil and oily fish, helps reduce cholesterol levels and inflammation, improving heart health.
- **Weight Management:** Due to its focus on whole, nutrient-dense foods, the Mediterranean diet supports healthy weight management. The high fibre content from fruits, vegetables, and whole grains promotes satiety, reducing the likelihood of overeating.
- **Reduced Risk of Diabetes:** The Mediterranean diet has been shown to improve insulin sensitivity and regulate blood sugar levels, making it an effective dietary approach for reducing the risk of Type 2 diabetes.
- **Improved Brain Health:** Research suggests that the Mediterranean diet may help protect against cognitive decline and neurodegenerative diseases such as Alzheimer's. The diet's antioxidant-rich foods and healthy fats are thought to support brain function and reduce oxidative stress.
- **Longevity:** Populations in Mediterranean regions, particularly in places like Crete and Sardinia, are known for their longevity and lower rates of age-related diseases. The combination of a balanced diet, physical activity, and a strong social support network contributes to a longer, healthier life.
- **Reduced Cancer Risk:** The diet's high intake of fruits, vegetables, and whole grains, combined with the consumption of antioxidant-rich foods, has been linked to a lower risk of certain cancers, including breast, colon, and

prostate cancer.
- **Better Gut Health:** The Mediterranean diet includes plenty of fibre from vegetables, legumes, and whole grains, promoting healthy digestion and supporting the gut microbiome. Fermented foods such as yoghurt and cheese also contribute to improved gut health.

Considerations and Precautions

While the Mediterranean diet is renowned for its many health benefits, there are some important considerations and precautions to bear in mind to ensure it is followed in a healthy and sustainable way:

- **Portion Control:** Despite the focus on healthy, whole foods, it is still important to maintain portion control, especially with calorie-dense items like olive oil, nuts, and seeds. Overconsumption can lead to weight gain.
- **Alcohol Consumption:** Moderate consumption of red wine is a characteristic of the Mediterranean diet, but it's important to consume alcohol responsibly. For individuals who do not drink, it's not necessary to start, as the health benefits of red wine can be obtained through other sources, such as grapes or berries.
- **Personalisation:** While the Mediterranean diet can be adapted to suit various lifestyles, it's important to personalise it based on individual health needs, preferences, and any underlying medical conditions. Consultation with a healthcare provider or nutritionist may be helpful for some.
- **Food Availability:** In some regions, the availability of fresh, seasonal ingredients may vary. Adapting the diet to include locally available, whole foods is still beneficial.

The Impact of the Mediterranean Diet

The Mediterranean diet's impact extends beyond individual health. It promotes a sustainable way of living that is beneficial to the environment. The diet's focus on plant-based foods and limited meat consumption aligns with sustainable food practices, reducing the carbon footprint associated with meat production. Furthermore, the Mediterranean diet encourages the use of locally sourced, seasonal produce, supporting local farmers and reducing food waste.

Additionally, the Mediterranean way of eating fosters a sense of community and social connection. Shared meals, whether with family or friends, create a supportive and joyful atmosphere that nourishes both body and soul. This holistic approach to well-being makes the Mediterranean diet a positive lifestyle choice, not just a temporary change in eating habits.

In summary, the Mediterranean diet is much more than just a way of eating—it's a lifestyle that emphasises balance, quality, and enjoyment. With its focus on whole foods, healthy fats, and mindful eating, it offers numerous health benefits, including improved heart health, weight management, and longevity. By following this diet, individuals can not only improve their physical well-being but also foster a greater sense of connection and joy in their relationship with food. The Mediterranean diet's rich history, scientific backing, and sustainable principles make it one of the most enduring and rewarding ways to maintain a healthy and fulfilling lifestyle.

Fundamentals of Mediterranean Diet

Fundamentals of Air Fryer

The air fryer has become increasingly popular in recent years, thanks to its ability to produce crispy, delicious meals with only a fraction of the oil typically used in traditional frying. In this recipe book, we're combining Mediterranean dishes with the convenience of the air fryer. To help you make the most of it, we'll introduce the air fryer in the following section, giving you a better understanding of how it works and why it's an ideal tool for preparing healthier Mediterranean recipes.

What is an Air Fryer?

An air fryer is a modern kitchen appliance that allows you to cook food by circulating hot air around it, giving it a crispy, fried-like texture without the need for excessive oil. It works through a convection mechanism, where a powerful fan circulates hot air at high speeds, cooking the food evenly from all angles. This process mimics the results of deep frying but uses significantly less oil, making it a healthier alternative.

The air fryer is particularly popular for preparing foods like chips, chicken, and fish, which traditionally require deep frying to achieve their signature crunch. In an air fryer, you can achieve that same crispy texture with just a small amount of oil—often as little as a teaspoon. The result is food with a golden, crisp exterior and a tender interior, but with fewer calories and less fat compared to deep frying.

Most air fryers come equipped with adjustable temperature settings and timers, allowing you to control the cooking process for different types of food. They are also versatile and can be used for roasting, baking, grilling, and even reheating leftovers. The compact design of the air fryer makes it more energy-efficient than traditional ovens, as it heats up more quickly and cooks food faster.

Cleaning up after using an air fryer is relatively easy, as many models feature non-stick, dishwasher-safe baskets and trays. This convenience, combined with its ability to produce healthier meals, has made the air fryer a staple in many households. Overall, an air fryer is a convenient, efficient, and health-conscious tool for those who enjoy fried foods but want to reduce their oil consumption.

Benefits of Using It

The air fryer has become a staple in many kitchens due to its versatility, efficiency, and health benefits. Whether you're cooking for yourself or a family, this appliance offers numerous advantages over traditional cooking methods. Below are ten unique benefits of using an air fryer, highlighting why it has earned its place in homes across the UK.

1. Healthier Cooking

One of the most well-known benefits of using an air fryer is its ability to cook food with significantly less oil than traditional frying methods. This makes it a healthier alternative, particularly for those looking to reduce their intake of unhealthy fats.

Air fryers use hot air circulation to cook food, often requiring only a light spray of oil or none at all. This allows you to enjoy crispy, fried-like foods with a lower calorie and fat content, making it easier to maintain a balanced diet.

2. Versatility in Cooking

An air fryer is not limited to frying; it can roast, grill, bake, and reheat a wide variety of dishes. This makes it a versatile appliance that can replace other kitchen gadgets, saving both space and money. From roasted vegetables and grilled chicken to baked goods and reheated leftovers, the air fryer's ability to handle multiple cooking techniques adds to its appeal. This versatility allows you to experiment with a range of dishes, from healthy snacks to indulgent desserts, all with minimal effort.

3. Energy Efficiency

Compared to traditional ovens, air fryers are much more energy-efficient. They preheat quickly and cook food faster due to their compact size and the rapid circulation of hot air. This can help reduce energy consumption and lower electricity bills, which is particularly beneficial in households where the oven is used frequently. Additionally, the quick cooking times mean you spend less time waiting for your meal, making it ideal for busy individuals or families.

4. Easy Clean-Up

Cleaning up after cooking can often be a tedious task, especially when using multiple pots, pans, or deep fryers. With an air fryer, clean-up is quick and easy. Most air fryers have removable baskets and trays that are non-stick and dishwasher-safe, making it a hassle-free process. Additionally, because air fryers use little to no oil, there is less grease to deal with compared to traditional frying, reducing the need for heavy scrubbing.

5. Consistent Cooking Results

One of the frustrations with traditional cooking methods is the inconsistency that can result from uneven heating. With an air fryer, hot air circulates evenly around the food, ensuring it cooks thoroughly on all sides. This means you can achieve consistent, reliable results every time, whether you're frying chips, baking pastries, or roasting vegetables. The even heat distribution also helps prevent burnt or undercooked spots, making your meals more enjoyable and presentable.

6. Compact and Space-Saving

Air fryers are typically compact and take up less counter space compared to other kitchen appliances, such as ovens or deep fryers. This makes them ideal for smaller kitchens or households with limited storage space. Despite their smaller size, many air fryers have a generous cooking capacity, allowing you to prepare meals for the whole family. Some models also come with dual-basket options, enabling you to cook two different dishes simultaneously, further increasing their convenience.

7. Safety Features

Air fryers are designed with safety in mind, making them a safer option than traditional frying methods, particularly deep frying. There is no need to handle large amounts of hot oil, reducing the risk of burns or kitchen fires. Many air fryers come equipped with automatic shut-off features, cool-to-the-touch exteriors, and locking lids, which enhance safety, especially in households with children. The appliance's enclosed design also minimises the risk of splattering oil or grease, making it a cleaner and safer cooking option overall.

8. Perfect for Reheating Leftovers

Air fryers excel at reheating food, offering a better alternative to microwaving. When reheating in a microwave, food can often become soggy or lose its original texture. In contrast, an air fryer reheats leftovers while maintaining or even enhancing their crispiness. Whether it's leftover pizza, chips, or roasted vegetables, the air fryer restores their original texture, making leftovers taste freshly cooked again. This feature is particularly useful for avoiding food waste, as it makes reheated meals more enjoyable.

Before First Use

Before using your air fryer for the first time, it's important to follow a few simple steps to ensure safe and optimal operation. These steps will prepare the appliance for use and help maintain its longevity.

- **Unbox the Appliance Carefully:** Remove the air fryer and all its components from the packaging. Ensure that no parts are missing or damaged during transit. Take out any accessories included, such as the basket, tray, or racks, and check the manual for any additional parts.
- **Remove All Packaging Materials:** Ensure that all plastic films, protective covers, and any packaging materials inside the appliance are completely removed. Check inside the basket and the cooking chamber for any hidden packaging or plastic.
- **Read the Instruction Manual:** Familiarise yourself with the user manual that comes with the air fryer. Each model can have slightly different features, so it's important to understand how yours operates, including its settings and safety precautions. Review the safety instructions, cooking presets, and maintenance tips to get the best results from your air fryer.

- **Clean the Accessories:** Before using your air fryer, wash the removable parts (basket, trays, racks) in warm, soapy water. Rinse them thoroughly and allow them to air-dry completely or use a clean towel. Most air fryer parts are dishwasher-safe, but refer to the manual to confirm if your model's accessories are suitable for dishwasher use.
- **Wipe Down the Exterior and Interior:** Using a soft, damp cloth, wipe the interior and exterior of the air fryer, including the control panel. Avoid using harsh cleaning agents or submerging the main unit in water, as this could damage the electrical components.
- **Preheat the Air Fryer:** Once your air fryer is clean and dry, plug it in and run a short preheat cycle at 180°C for 5-10 minutes. This will burn off any factory residues and eliminate any initial odours. Allow the air fryer to cool down completely before proceeding with the first cooking session.
- **Find a Suitable Location:** Ensure the air fryer is placed on a flat, stable surface with adequate ventilation. Leave at least 10 cm of space around the appliance to allow proper air circulation while cooking.

After completing these steps, your air fryer will be ready for use, and you can start enjoying healthier, crispier meals.

Step-By-Step Guide

Using an air fryer is a simple and convenient way to cook healthier meals. Follow these steps to make the most of your appliance:

1. Read the Instruction Manual

Before using the air fryer, read the manual that comes with it. Each model may have different features, so understanding your appliance is crucial for optimal use.

2. Prepare Your Ingredients

Prepare your food by cutting, seasoning, or marinating as necessary. Lightly coat ingredients with a small amount of oil if required to achieve a crispy texture. Avoid overcrowding the basket for even cooking.

3. Preheat the Air Fryer (If Necessary)

Some air fryers require preheating. Set the desired temperature and let the unit preheat for 3-5 minutes, if recommended by your manual.

4. Load the Basket

Place the food evenly in the air fryer basket. Make sure the pieces are spread out to allow hot air to circulate properly. For larger portions, cook in batches to prevent overcrowding.

5. Set Temperature and Time

Adjust the temperature and cooking time according to your recipe. Air fryers usually range between 80°C and 200°C. Many models come with presets for different types of food, but you can always set the time manually.

6. Shake or Flip Food Midway

For even cooking, shake the basket or flip the food halfway through the cooking time. Most air fryers automatically pause when the basket is removed and resume once it is returned.

7. Check for Doneness

Once the cooking time is up, carefully remove the basket and check if the food is cooked to your liking. If more time is needed, return the basket and cook for a few more minutes.

8. Clean the Air Fryer

After the air fryer has cooled down, clean the basket, tray, and any removable parts with warm soapy water. Many of these components are dishwasher-safe. Wipe down the exterior with a damp cloth.

By following these simple steps, you can enjoy delicious, healthy meals with minimal effort using your air fryer.

Tips for Using Accessories

Using the right accessories with your air fryer can enhance its versatility and make cooking even more efficient. Here are some tips for getting the most out of your air fryer accessories:

- **Use the Rack for Multiple Layers:** Many air fryers come with a rack that allows you to cook food on two levels. This is ideal for preparing larger portions or different foods simultaneously, ensuring everything cooks evenly without overcrowding the basket.
- **Silicone Mats and Baking Cups:** Using silicone mats or baking cups can help prevent food from sticking to the basket, making clean-up easier. They are especially useful for cooking delicate items like baked goods or eggs.
- **Parchment Paper:** If you're frying foods like fish or vegetables, placing a sheet of air fryer-friendly parchment paper under the food can absorb excess grease and prevent sticking. Ensure the parchment paper is perforated to allow proper air circulation.
- **Cooking Tongs:** Invest in silicone-tipped tongs to safely handle hot food without scratching the non-stick surface of the air fryer basket.
- **Dishwasher-Safe Accessories:** Always check that your accessories are dishwasher-safe to save time on cleaning. Avoid using accessories with metal parts that may damage the non-stick coating.

By using these accessories correctly, you can improve your air frying experience and extend the life of your appliance.

Cleaning and Caring for an Air Fryer

Proper cleaning and care of your air fryer will ensure its

| Fundamentals of Mediterranean Diet

longevity and continued performance. Here's how to keep your air fryer in top condition:

- **Clean After Every Use:** After each use, allow the air fryer to cool completely before cleaning. Remove the basket, tray, and any other removable parts. These are often dishwasher-safe, but you can also wash them by hand using warm soapy water. Avoid using abrasive sponges that could damage the non-stick coating.
- **Wipe Down the Interior:** Use a soft, damp cloth to wipe the inside of the air fryer. Ensure no food residue or grease is left behind. Be careful around the heating element and avoid submerging the main unit in water.
- **Clean the Exterior:** Regularly wipe down the outside of the air fryer with a cloth to keep it free of dust, grease, and fingerprints. Make sure the control panel is clean, but avoid getting it too wet.
- **Descale If Necessary:** Over time, some models may build up residue from repeated cooking. If this occurs, use a mixture of water and vinegar to gently clean these areas.
- **Air Dry Completely:** Ensure all parts are fully dry before reassembling the air fryer. Storing it with any moisture can damage the unit.

By cleaning and caring for your air fryer after each use, you can maintain its functionality and keep it working efficiently for years to come.

Frequently Asked Questions Preparation

1. Do I need to preheat the air fryer?

Some air fryer models require preheating, while others do not. Check your user manual for guidance. Preheating can help ensure even cooking, particularly for crispier results.

2. Can I cook frozen food in an air fryer?

Yes, air fryers are great for cooking frozen foods such as chips, nuggets, and fish fillets. You can cook them straight from frozen without needing to thaw.

3. Do I need to use oil in an air fryer?

While an air fryer can cook food with little to no oil, a light spray of oil can enhance the crispiness of certain foods like chips or chicken wings. However, it uses far less oil than traditional frying methods.

4. Can I cook multiple foods at once?

Yes, many air fryers come with a rack that allows you to cook different foods simultaneously. Just make sure not to overcrowd the basket for even cooking.

5. Is the air fryer easy to clean?

Most air fryer parts, such as the basket and tray, are dishwasher-safe. Alternatively, you can wash them by hand with warm soapy water. Always clean after each use to maintain hygiene and performance.

4-Week Meal Plan

Week 1

Day 1:
Breakfast: Keto Courgette Muffins
Lunch: Tabbouleh Stuffed Tomatoes
Snack: Easy Air Fryer Popcorn
Dinner: Provencal Salmon Fillets
Dessert: Poached Pears in Red Wine Sauce

Day 2:
Breakfast: Easy Harissa Shakshuka
Lunch: Roasted Vegetable Mélange
Snack: Greek Yoghurt Deviled Eggs
Dinner: Crispy Breaded Turkey Cutlets
Dessert: Raspberry Meringues

Day 3:
Breakfast: Cheesy Spinach and Egg Pie
Lunch: Honey Glazed Carrots with Walnuts
Snack: Goat Cheese Crostini with Basil
Dinner: Roasted Beef Tips with Yellow Onions
Dessert: Chocolate Molten Lava Cake

Day 4:
Breakfast: Sweet Potato Toast with Vegetables and Eggs
Lunch: Perfect Mediterranean Veggie Pizza
Snack: Air Fried Crab Cakes
Dinner: Steamed Cod with Onions & Swiss Chard
Dessert: Cinnamon Baked Apples with Walnuts

Day 5:
Breakfast: Crispy Honey Nut Granola
Lunch: Roasted Cauliflower Steaks with Baba Ghanoush
Snack: Crunchy Turmeric Roasted Chickpeas
Dinner: Crispy Chicken Tenders
Dessert: Pistachio Butter Cookies

Day 6:
Breakfast: Air Fryer Ramekin Eggs
Lunch: Roasted Brussels Sprouts Salad with Almonds
Snack: Chinese Five-Spice Flavoured Popcorn
Dinner: Greek Beef Meatloaf
Dessert: Classic Crème Caramel

Day 7:
Breakfast: Chard and Feta Frittata
Lunch: Crispy Artichoke Hearts
Snack: Roasted Mini Potatoes
Dinner: Roasted Pork Tenderloin and Lemony Orzo
Dessert: Crispy Baklava with Walnuts

Week 2

Day 1:
Breakfast: Avocado Toast with Poached Eggs
Lunch: Star Anise-Glazed Carrots
Snack: Crispy Pita Wedges
Dinner: Crispy Polenta Fish Sticks
Dessert: Crispy Cinnamon Sugar Biscotti

Day 2:
Breakfast: Ramekin Baked Eggs with Swiss Chard, Feta, and Basil
Lunch: Roasted Grape Tomatoes and Asparagus
Snack: Tasty Moroccan Courgette Spread
Dinner: Sumac Roasted Chicken with Cauliflower and Carrots
Dessert: Semolina and Syrup Cake

Day 3:
Breakfast: Mixed Berry Baked Oatmeal
Lunch: Pesto Pita Pizza with Mushrooms
Snack: Lemon Cauliflower with Saffron Dipping Sauce
Dinner: Simple Lamb Meatballs
Dessert: French Cherry Clafoutis

Day 4:
Breakfast: Healthy Greek Yoghurt Parfait with Granola
Lunch: Lemon Tofu with Sun-Dried Tomatoes and Artichokes
Snack: Mashed Fava Beans Crostini
Dinner: Salmon with Orange and Dill
Dessert: Poached Pears in Red Wine Sauce

Day 5:
Breakfast: Mini Carrot Bran Muffins
Lunch: Roasted Tomato, Aubergine, and Chickpeas
Snack: Healthy Trail Mix
Dinner: Herb Roasted Whole Chicken
Dessert: Raspberry Meringues

Day 6:
Breakfast: Homemade Olive Tapenade Flatbread
Lunch: Parmesan and Thyme Roasted Butternut Squash
Snack: Easy Air Fryer Popcorn
Dinner: Sriracha Lamb Chops
Dessert: Cinnamon Baked Apples with Walnuts

Day 7:
Breakfast: Fluffy Cheese Pancake
Lunch: Crispy Aubergine Slices
Snack: Greek Yoghurt Deviled Eggs
Dinner: Pork Roast with Apple Dijon Sauce
Dessert: Chocolate Molten Lava Cake

Week 3

Day 1:
Breakfast: Cheesy Spinach and Egg Pie
Lunch: Roasted Beets with Fresh Dill
Snack: Air Fried Crab Cakes
Dinner: Garlic Shrimp and Mushroom Pasta
Dessert: Crispy Baklava with Walnuts

Day 2:
Breakfast: Keto Courgette Muffins
Lunch: Roasted Broccoli Florets with Orange
Snack: Goat Cheese Crostini with Basil
Dinner: Rosemary Roasted Chicken Drumsticks
Dessert: Pistachio Butter Cookies

Day 3:
Breakfast: Easy Harissa Shakshuka
Lunch: White Clam Pizza Pie
Snack: Crunchy Turmeric Roasted Chickpeas
Dinner: Mini Greek Meatloaves
Dessert: Classic Crème Caramel

Day 4:
Breakfast: Sweet Potato Toast with Vegetables and Eggs
Lunch: Tabbouleh Stuffed Tomatoes
Snack: Crispy Pita Wedges
Dinner: Foil Baked Fish with Garlic
Dessert: Crispy Cinnamon Sugar Biscotti

Day 5:
Breakfast: Crispy Honey Nut Granola
Lunch: Roasted Vegetable Mélange
Snack: Chinese Five-Spice Flavoured Popcorn
Dinner: Classic Chicken Kebab with Vegetables
Dessert: Semolina and Syrup Cake

Day 6:
Breakfast: Air Fryer Ramekin Eggs
Lunch: Honey Glazed Carrots with Walnuts
Snack: Roasted Mini Potatoes
Dinner: Herbed Dijon Roasted Pork Tenderloin
Dessert: French Cherry Clafoutis

Day 7:
Breakfast: Chard and Feta Frittata
Lunch: Roasted Cauliflower Steaks with Baba Ghanoush
Snack: Tasty Moroccan Courgette Spread
Dinner: Authentic Greek Moussaka
Dessert: Poached Pears in Red Wine Sauce

Week 4

Day 1:
Breakfast: Avocado Toast with Poached Eggs
Lunch: Roasted Brussels Sprouts Salad with Almonds
Snack: Mashed Fava Beans Crostini
Dinner: Roasted Fish Fillets with Green Beans and Tomatoes
Dessert: Raspberry Meringues

Day 2:
Breakfast: Mixed Berry Baked Oatmeal
Lunch: Star Anise-Glazed Carrots
Snack: Lemon Cauliflower with Saffron Dipping Sauce
Dinner: Air Fried Turkey Meatballs
Dessert: Cinnamon Baked Apples with Walnuts

Day 3:
Breakfast: Ramekin Baked Eggs with Swiss Chard, Feta, and Basil
Lunch: Chicken Artichoke Pizza with Olives
Snack: Healthy Trail Mix
Dinner: Homemade Greek Meatballs (Keftedes)
Dessert: Chocolate Molten Lava Cake

Day 4:
Breakfast: Healthy Greek Yoghurt Parfait with Granola
Lunch: Roasted Grape Tomatoes and Asparagus
Snack: Easy Air Fryer Popcorn
Dinner: Honey Glazed Salmon Fillets
Dessert: Pistachio Butter Cookies

Day 5:
Breakfast: Mini Carrot Bran Muffins
Lunch: Roasted Tomato, Aubergine, and Chickpeas
Snack: Greek Yoghurt Deviled Eggs
Dinner: Chicken Kebabs with Tzatziki Sauce
Dessert: Crispy Baklava with Walnuts

Day 6:
Breakfast: Homemade Olive Tapenade Flatbread
Lunch: Parmesan and Thyme Roasted Butternut Squash
Snack: Air Fried Crab Cakes
Dinner: Lemon Garlic Chicken Thighs
Dessert: Classic Crème Caramel

Day 7:
Breakfast: Fluffy Cheese Pancake
Lunch: Roasted Broccoli Florets with Orange
Snack: Crunchy Turmeric Roasted Chickpeas
Dinner: Roasted Halibut in Parchment with Courgette and Thyme
Dessert: Crispy Cinnamon Sugar Biscotti

Chapter 1 Breakfast

Easy Harissa Shakshuka 15
Keto Courgette Muffins 15
Cheesy Spinach and Egg Pie 16
Sweet Potato Toast with Vegetables and Eggs 16
Crispy Honey Nut Granola 17
Air Fryer Ramekin Eggs 17
Chard and Feta Frittata 18
Avocado Toast with Poached Eggs 18
Ramekin Baked Eggs with Swiss Chard, Feta, and Basil ... 19
Mixed Berry Baked Oatmeal 19
Healthy Greek Yoghurt Parfait with Granola 20
Mini Carrot Bran Muffins 20
Homemade Olive Tapenade Flatbread 21
Fluffy Cheese Pancake 21

Easy Harissa Shakshuka

⏱ Prep: 10 minutes   🍳 Cook: 20 minutes   🍽 Serves: 4

Ingredients:

1½ tablespoons extra-virgin olive oil
2 tablespoons harissa
1 tablespoon tomato paste
½ onion, diced
1 bell pepper, seeded and diced
3 garlic cloves, minced
1 (795g) can no-salt-added diced tomatoes
½ teaspoon kosher salt
4 large eggs
2 to 3 tablespoons fresh basil, chopped or cut into ribbons

Preparation:

1. In a 12-inch cast-iron pan or ovenproof skillet over medium heat, heat the olive oil. Add the harissa, onion, tomato paste, and bell pepper, and sauté for 3 to 4 minutes. Add the garlic and cook until fragrant, about 30 seconds. Add the diced tomatoes and salt and simmer for about 10 minutes. 2. Make 4 wells in the sauce and gently break 1 egg into each. Transfer the pan to the air fryer and cook at 190°C until the whites are cooked and the yolks are set, 10 to 12 minutes. 3. Allow to cool for 3 to 5 minutes, garnish with the basil, and carefully spoon onto plates.

Per Serving: Calories 165; Fat 10.4g; Sodium 386mg; Carbs 11.13g; Fibre 4.4g; Sugar 6.92g; Protein 8.58g

Keto Courgette Muffins

⏱ Prep: 15 minutes   🍳 Cook: 20 minutes   🍽 Serves: 4

Ingredients:

Nonstick cooking spray
185g shredded courgette
2 eggs
85g honey
3 tablespoons extra-virgin olive oil
1 tablespoon orange zest
1 teaspoon pure vanilla extract
120g whole-wheat flour
110g almond flour
2 teaspoons baking powder
1 teaspoon baking soda
1 teaspoon ground cinnamon
1 teaspoon salt
60g chopped walnuts (optional)

Preparation:

1. Spray a 12-muffin pan with nonstick cooking spray. 2. In a medium bowl, combine the courgette, honey, eggs, and olive oil and stir well. 3. Add the orange zest, wheat and almond flours, baking powder, vanilla extract, baking soda, cinnamon, and salt, and mix well. 4. Fold in the chopped walnuts (if using). 5. Scoop the batter into the prepared muffin pan. 6. Place the pan into the air fryer and bake at 190°C 15 to 20 minutes or until the muffins are lightly browned. Cool for 5 minutes in the pan and remove. 7. Store the muffins in a tightly sealed container for several days at room temperature, or freeze for several months.

Per Serving: Calories 371; Fat 19.86g; Sodium 935mg; Carbs 44.27g; Fibre 4.8g; Sugar 19.42g; Protein 8.94g

Chapter 1 Breakfast

Cheesy Spinach and Egg Pie

⏰ **Prep:** 10 minutes 🍲 **Cook:** 25 minutes 🍽 **Serves:** 8

Ingredients:

Nonstick cooking spray
2 tablespoons extra-virgin olive oil
1 onion, chopped
455g frozen spinach, thawed
¼ teaspoon garlic salt
¼ teaspoon freshly ground black pepper
¼ teaspoon ground nutmeg
4 large eggs, divided
100g grated Parmesan cheese, divided
2 puff pastry doughs (organic, if available), at room temperature
4 hard-boiled eggs, halved

Preparation:

1. Spray a baking pan that fits your air fryer with the nonstick cooking spray and set aside. 2. Heat a large sauté pan or skillet over medium-high heat. Put in the oil and onion and cook for about 5 minutes, until translucent. 3. Squeeze the excess water from the spinach, add to the pan and cook, uncovered, so that any excess water from the spinach can evaporate. Add the garlic, salt, pepper, and nutmeg. Remove from heat and set aside to cool. 4. In a small bowl, crack 3 eggs and mix well. Add the eggs and 50g Parmesan cheese to the cooled spinach mix. 5. On the prepared baking pan, roll out the pastry dough. Layer the spinach mix on top of the dough, leaving 2 inches around each edge. 6. Once the spinach is spread onto the pastry dough, place hard-boiled egg halves evenly throughout the pie, then cover with the second pastry dough. Pinch the edges closed. 7. Crack the remaining egg in a small bowl and mix well. Brush the egg wash over the pastry dough. 8. Place the baking pan in the air fryer basket and cook at 175°C for 15 to 20 minutes, until golden brown and warmed through. 9. When done, serve and enjoy.

Per Serving: Calories 231; Fat 15.57g; Sodium 360mg; Carbs 10.57g; Fibre 2.1g; Sugar 1.41g; Protein 12.81g

Sweet Potato Toast with Vegetables and Eggs

⏰ **Prep:** 5 minutes 🍲 **Cook:** 15 minutes 🍽 **Serves:** 4

Ingredients:

2 plum tomatoes, halved
6 tablespoons extra-virgin olive oil, divided
Salt
Freshly ground black pepper
2 large sweet potatoes, sliced lengthwise
30g fresh spinach
8 medium asparagus, trimmed
4 large cooked eggs or egg substitute (poached, scrambled, or fried)
20g arugula
4 tablespoons pesto
4 tablespoons shredded Asiago cheese

Preparation:

1. Brush the plum tomato halves with 2 tablespoons of olive oil and season with the salt and pepper. 2. Place the plum tomato halves in the air fryer basket and roast the tomatoes at 230°C for approximately 15 minutes, then remove from the air fryer and allow to rest. 3. Brush the sweet potato slices with about 2 tablespoons of oil on each side and season with salt and pepper. 4. Arrange the sweet potato slices in the air fryer basket and cook the sweet potato slices for about 15 minutes, flipping once after 5 to 7 minutes, until just tender. Remove from the air fryer and set aside. 5. In a sauté pan or skillet, heat the remaining 2 tablespoons of olive oil over medium heat and sauté the fresh spinach until just wilted. Remove from the pan and rest on a paper-towel-lined dish. In the same pan, add the asparagus and sauté, turning throughout. Transfer to a paper towel-lined dish. 6. Place the slices of grilled sweet potato on serving plates and divide the spinach and asparagus evenly among the slices. Place a prepared egg on top of the spinach and asparagus. Top this with 20g of arugula. 7. Finish by drizzling with 1 tablespoon of pesto and sprinkle with 1 tablespoon of cheese. Serve with 1 roasted plum tomato.

Per Serving: Calories 480; Fat 39.35g; Sodium 822mg; Carbs 21.09g; Fibre 3.6g; Sugar 8.16g; Protein 12.66g

Crispy Honey Nut Granola

⏱ Prep: 10 minutes   🍳 Cook: 20 minutes   ≋ Serves: 6

Ingredients:
210g regular rolled oats
40g coarsely chopped almonds
⅛ teaspoon kosher or sea salt
½ teaspoon ground cinnamon
80g chopped dried apricots
2 tablespoons ground flaxseed
85g honey
60ml extra-virgin olive oil
2 teaspoons vanilla extract

Preparation:
1. Line the air fryer basket with parchment paper. 2. In a large skillet, combine the oats, almonds, salt, and cinnamon. Turn the heat to medium-high and cook, stirring often, to toast, about 6 minutes. 3. While the oat mixture is cooking, in a microwave-safe bowl, combine the apricots, flaxseed, honey, and oil. Microwave on high for about 1 minute, or until very hot and just beginning to bubble. 4. Stir the vanilla into the honey mixture, then pour it over the oat mixture in the skillet. Stir well. 5. Spread out the granola to the air fryer basket and bake at 160°C for 15 minutes, until lightly browned. Remove from the air fryer and cool completely. 6. Break the granola into the small pieces and store in an airtight container in the refrigerator for up to 2 weeks (if it lasts that long!).
Per Serving: Calories 330; Fat 15.32g; Sodium 57mg; Carbs 43.75g; Fibre 5.9g; Sugar 18.19g; Protein 6.59g

Air Fryer Ramekin Eggs

⏱ Prep: 10 minutes   🍳 Cook: 5-10 minutes   ≋ Serves: 4

Ingredients:
4 teaspoons extra-virgin olive oil
8 eggs
50g grated Parmesan cheese
1 teaspoon salt
¼ teaspoon freshly ground black pepper

Preparation:
1. Place 1 teaspoon of olive oil in each of the four ramekins and tilt to coat the ramekin with the oil. 2. Carefully break two eggs into each ramekin. You can break one egg in each ramekin if desired. 3. Divide the Parmesan cheese among the four ramekins. 4. Season each ramekin with the salt and pepper. 5. Place the ramekins into the air fryer and cook at 200°C for 5 to 10 minutes, depending on how runny or hard you like your yolks. 6. When done, serve immediately.
Per Serving: Calories 219; Fat 16.35g; Sodium 932mg; Carbs 2.48g; Fibre 0g; Sugar 0.34g; Protein 14.62g

Chard and Feta Frittata

⏱ **Prep: 15 minutes** 🍲 **Cook: 25 minutes** ❖ **Serves: 6**

Ingredients:

1 tablespoon extra-virgin olive oil
1 bunch chard, stems removed, leaves coarsely chopped
1 teaspoon salt
¼ teaspoon freshly ground black pepper
80g chopped roasted red peppers
60g chopped olives
1 teaspoon dried oregano
12 eggs, well-beaten
55g crumbled feta cheese

Preparation:

1. Place the olive oil in a sided pie plate. 2. Add the chopped chard, salt, and pepper. 3. Place the pie plate in the air fryer and cook at 190°C for 10 to 15 minutes, or until the chard is wilted. 4. Remove from the air fryer and sprinkle the roasted red pepper, olives, and oregano over the chard. 5. Carefully pour the beaten eggs into the pie plate. Scatter the feta over the eggs. 6. Return the pie plate to the air fryer and bake at 190°C for 20 to 25 minutes, or until the eggs are just set and they still jiggle a bit when moved. 7. Let it cool for 5 minutes before serving. Cut into the wedges and serve. 8. The frittata will last, covered in the refrigerator, for one week. You can freeze frittatas for several months, but when thawed, they have a tendency to be runny.

Per Serving: Calories 194; Fat 13.4g; Sodium 802mg; Carbs 4.77g; Fibre 1.6g; Sugar 1.8g; Protein 13.88g

Avocado Toast with Poached Eggs

⏱ **Prep: 5 minutes** 🍲 **Cook: 7 minutes** ❖ **Serves: 4**

Ingredients:

Olive oil cooking spray
4 large eggs
Salt
Black pepper
4 pieces whole grain bread
1 avocado
Red pepper flakes (optional)

Preparation:

1. Lightly coat the inside of four small oven-safe ramekins with olive oil cooking spray. 2. Crack one egg into each ramekin, and season with salt and black pepper. 3. Place the ramekins into the air fryer basket and cook at 160°C for 7 minutes. 4. While the eggs are cooking, toast the bread in a toaster. 5. Slice the avocado in half lengthwise, remove the pit, and scoop the flesh into a small bowl. Season with the salt, black pepper, and red pepper flakes, if desired. Using a fork, smash the avocado lightly. 6. Spread a quarter of the smashed avocado evenly over each slice of toast. 7. Remove the eggs from the air fryer and gently spoon one onto each slice of avocado toast before serving.

Per Serving: Calories 227; Fat 13.34g; Sodium 465mg; Carbs 17.11g; Fibre 5.5g; Sugar 2.78g; Protein 11g

Ramekin Baked Eggs with Swiss Chard, Feta, and Basil

⏰ Prep: 15 minutes 🍲 Cook: 10-15 minutes 🍽 Serves: 4

Ingredients:

1 tablespoon extra-virgin olive oil, divided
½ red onion, diced
½ teaspoon kosher salt
¼ teaspoon nutmeg
⅛ teaspoon freshly ground black pepper
145g Swiss chard, chopped
30g crumbled feta cheese
4 large eggs
5g fresh basil, chopped or cut into ribbons

Preparation:

1. Grease 4 ramekins lightly with the olive oil. 2. Heat the remaining olive oil in a large sauté pan or skillet over medium heat. Add the salt, onion, nutmeg, and pepper and sauté until translucent, about 3 minutes. Add the chard and cook, stirring, until wilted, about 2 minutes. 3. Split the mixture among the 4 ramekins. Add 1 tablespoon feta cheese to each ramekin. Crack 1 egg on top of the mixture in each ramekin. Arrange the ramekins in the air fryer basket and bake at 190°C for 10 to 12 minutes or until the egg white is set. 4. Allow to cool for 1 to 2 minutes, then carefully transfer the eggs from the ramekins to a plate with a fork or spatula. Garnish with the basil.

Per Serving: Calories 140; Fat 10.28g; Sodium 525mg; Carbs 3.55g; Fibre 0.9g; Sugar 1.56g; Protein 8.48g

Mixed Berry Baked Oatmeal

⏰ Prep: 10 minutes 🍲 Cook: 45-50 minutes 🍽 Serves: 8

Ingredients:

165g gluten-free rolled oats
285g frozen mixed berries (blueberries and raspberries work best)
470ml plain, unsweetened almond milk
245g plain Greek yoghurt
60ml maple syrup
2 tablespoons extra-virgin olive oil
2 teaspoons ground cinnamon
1 teaspoon baking powder
1 teaspoon vanilla extract
½ teaspoon kosher salt
¼ teaspoon ground nutmeg
⅛ teaspoon ground cloves

Preparation:

1. Combine all the ingredients together in a large bowl. Pour into a baking dish. 2. Place the baking dish into the air fryer and bake at 190°C for 45 to 50 minutes or until golden brown. 3. When done, serve and enjoy.

Per Serving: Calories 210; Fat 8.51g; Sodium 191mg; Carbs 35.99g; Fibre 5.9g; Sugar 16.65g; Protein 7.59g

Healthy Greek Yoghurt Parfait with Granola

⏰ **Prep: 10 minutes** 🍲 **Cook: 30 minutes** 📚 **Serves: 4**

Ingredients:

For the Granola:
85g honey or maple syrup
2 tablespoons vegetable oil
2 teaspoons vanilla extract
½ teaspoon kosher salt
250g gluten-free rolled oats
120g mixed raw and unsalted nuts, chopped
35g sunflower seeds
160g unsweetened dried cherries

For the Parfait:
490g plain Greek yoghurt
150g fresh fruit, chopped (optional)

Preparation:

To make the granola: 1. Line the air fryer basket with parchment paper or foil. 2. Heat the honey, vanilla, oil, and salt in a small saucepan over medium heat. Simmer for 2 minutes and stir together well. 3. In a large bowl, combine the nuts, oats, and seeds. Pour the warm oil mixture over the top and toss well. Spread the mixture in a single layer in the air fryer basket. Bake at 160°C for 30 minutes, stirring halfway through. 4. Remove from the air fryer and add in the dried cherries. Cool completely and store in an airtight container at room temperature for up to 3 months.

To make the parfait: 1. For one serving: In a bowl or lowball drinking glass, spoon in 120g yoghurt, 60g granola, and 40g fruit (if desired). Layer in whatever pattern you like.

Per Serving: Calories 634; Fat 36.19g; Sodium 363mg; Carbs 84.27g; Fibre 13.3g; Sugar 25.49g; Protein 23.99g

Mini Carrot Bran Muffins

⏰ **Prep: 10 minutes** 🍲 **Cook: 18 minutes** 📚 **Serves: 6**

Ingredients:

Nonstick cooking spray
95g oat bran
120g whole-wheat flour
65g all-purpose flour
40g old-fashioned oats
3 tablespoons packed brown sugar
1 teaspoon baking soda
1 teaspoon baking powder
2 teaspoons ground cinnamon
2 teaspoons ground ginger
½ teaspoon ground nutmeg
¼ teaspoon sea salt
300ml unsweetened almond milk
2 tablespoons honey
1 egg
2 tablespoons extra-virgin olive oil
165g grated carrots
35g raisins

Preparation:

1. Line two mini muffin tins with paper liners or coat them with nonstick cooking spray. 2. In a large bowl, whisk the oat bran, oats, brown sugar, whole-wheat and all-purpose flours, baking soda, baking powder, ginger, nutmeg, cinnamon, and salt. Set aside. 3. In a medium bowl, whisk the egg, almond milk, honey, and olive oil. 4. Add the wet ingredients to the dry ingredients and fold until just blended. The batter will be lumpy with streaks of flour remaining. 5. Fold in the carrots and raisins. 6. Fill each muffin cup three-fourths full. Working in batches, place the mini muffin into the air fryer and bake at 175°C for 15 to 18 minutes until a toothpick inserted in the centre of a muffin comes out clean. 7. Cool on a wire rack before serving.

Per Serving: Calories 293; Fat 8.29g; Sodium 375mg; Carbs 56.67g; Fibre 7.6g; Sugar 15.87g; Protein 9.4g

| Chapter 1 Breakfast

Homemade Olive Tapenade Flatbread

⏱ **Prep: 30 minutes**   🍲 **Cook: 5 minutes**   ❖ **Serves: 6**

Ingredients:

For the Flatbread:
180ml warm water (50°C)
1 tablespoon honey
1 package quick-rising yeast
90g whole-wheat flour, plus more for dusting the work surface
30g all-purpose flour
½ teaspoon sea salt
1 tablespoon extra-virgin olive oil

For the Tapenade:
120g black olives, pitted and chopped
120g green olives, pitted and chopped
2 roasted red pepper slices, chopped
1 tablespoon capers, drained and rinsed
1 garlic clove, minced
1 tablespoon chopped fresh basil leaves
1 tablespoon chopped fresh oregano leaves
60ml extra-virgin olive oil

Preparation:

To make the flatbread: 1. In a small bowl, whisk the water, honey, and yeast. Let stand for about 5 minutes, covered with a clean kitchen towel, until the yeast foams. 2. In a large bowl, whisk the whole-wheat and all-purpose flours and sea salt. Add the yeast mixture and stir until a ball forms. 3. Turn the dough out onto a floured surface and knead for about 5 minutes until smooth. 4. Brush a bowl with the olive oil. Add the dough and turn to coat with the oil. Cover and place in a warm spot to rise for about 1 hour until doubled. 5. Split the dough into 6 portions. Roll each into a thin oblong shape, ¼ to ½ inch thick. 6. Place the flatbreads in the air fryer basket and bake at 200°C for about 5 minutes until browned.

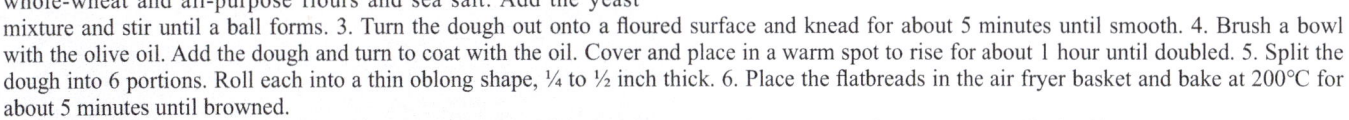

To make the tapenade: 1. In a food processor or blender, mix together the black and green olives, capers, garlic, basil, roasted pepper, oregano, and olive oil. Process for 10 to 20 (1-second) pulses until coarsely chopped.

Per Serving: Calories 147; Fat 5.78g; Sodium mg; Carbs 22.42g; Fibre 495g; Sugar 5.26g; Protein 3.34g

Fluffy Cheese Pancake

⏱ **Prep: 30 minutes**   🍲 **Cook: 30 minutes**   ❖ **Serves: 3-5**

Ingredients:
240ml water
2 large eggs
1 teaspoon honey
1 teaspoon olive oil
95g all-purpose flour
2 tablespoons unsalted butter, melted
Freshly ground black pepper
170g feta, crumbled, divided
1 tablespoon honey, for drizzling

Preparation:

1. Line the air fryer basket with parchment paper. 2. In a medium bowl, whisk together the water, honey, eggs, and olive oil until well combined. 3. Add the flour and melted butter and stir until well blended. Season with the pepper. Cover the batter and let stand for 20 minutes or until it thickens a bit. 4. Stir 115g of feta into the batter, then pour the batter into the centre of the prepared basket (it will spread out into a circle) and sprinkle evenly with the remaining 55g of feta. 5. Bake at 200°C for 25 to 30 minutes, until golden brown. 6. Remove the pancake from the air fryer and cut the pancake into 3-inch squares or to the size and shape you prefer. 7. Serve drizzled with the honey.

Per Serving: Calories 300; Fat 16.64g; Sodium 430mg; Carbs 25.7g; Fibre 0.7g; Sugar 7.66g; Protein 11.87g

Chapter 1 Breakfast | 21

Chapter 2 Vegetarian Mains

Tabbouleh Stuffed Tomatoes 23
Roasted Vegetable Mélange 23
Honey Glazed Carrots with Walnuts 24
Roasted Cauliflower Steaks with Baba Ghanoush 24
Roasted Brussels Sprouts Salad with Almonds 25
Star Anise-Glazed Carrots 25
Crispy Artichoke Hearts 26
Roasted Grape Tomatoes and Asparagus 26
Lemon Tofu with Sun-Dried Tomatoes and Artichokes 27
Roasted Tomato, Aubergine, and Chickpeas 27
Parmesan and Thyme Roasted Butternut Squash 28
Crispy Aubergine Slices 28
Roasted Beets with Fresh Dill 29
Roasted Broccoli Florets with Orange 29

Tabbouleh Stuffed Tomatoes

⏰ **Prep: 10 minutes**   🍲 **Cook: 20 minutes**   🍽 **Serves: 4**

Ingredients:

8 medium beefsteak or similar tomatoes
3 tablespoons extra-virgin olive oil, divided
120ml water
120g uncooked regular or whole-wheat couscous
90g minced fresh curly parsley (about 1 large bunch)
20g minced fresh mint
2 scallions, green and white parts, chopped (about 2 tablespoons)
¼ teaspoon freshly ground black pepper
¼ teaspoon kosher or sea salt
1 medium lemon
4 teaspoons honey
40g chopped almonds

Preparation:

1. Slice the top off each tomato and set aside. Scoop out all the flesh inside, and put the tops, flesh, and seeds in a large mixing bowl. 2. Grease the air fryer basket with 1 tablespoon of oil. Place the carved-out tomatoes in the air fryer basket and roast at 200°C for 10 minutes. 3. While the tomatoes are cooking, make the couscous by bringing the water to boil in a medium saucepan. Pour in the couscous, remove from the heat, and cover. Let sit for 5 minutes, and then stir with a fork. 4. While the couscous is cooking, chop up the tomato flesh and tops. Drain off the excess tomato water using a colander. Measure out 250g of the chopped tomatoes (reserve any remaining chopped tomatoes for another use). Add the cup of tomatoes back into the mixing bowl. Mix in the parsley, mint, pepper, scallions, and salt. 5. Using a Microplane or citrus grater, zest the lemon into the mixing bowl. Halve the lemon and squeeze the juice through a strainer (to catch the seeds) from both halves into the bowl with the tomato mixture. Mix well. 6. When the couscous is ready, add it to the tomato mixture and mix well. 7. With oven mitts, carefully remove the tomatoes from the air fryer. Divide the tabbouleh evenly among the tomatoes and stuff them, using a spoon to press the filling down so it all fits. Return the tomatoes to the air fryer and cook for another 8 to 10 minutes or until the tomatoes are tender-firm. If you prefer softer tomatoes, roast for an additional 10 minutes. Before serving, top each tomato with a drizzle of ½ teaspoon of honey and about 2 teaspoons of almonds.
Per Serving: Calories 259; Fat 16.83g; Sodium 173mg; Carbs 25.48g; Fibre 5.9g; Sugar 13.58g; Protein 6.48g

Roasted Vegetable Mélange

⏰ **Prep: 20 minutes**   🍲 **Cook: 25 minutes**   🍽 **Serves: 4**

Ingredients:

½ cauliflower head, cut into small florets
½ broccoli head, cut into small florets
2 courgette, cut into ½-inch pieces
140g halved mushrooms
2 red, orange, or yellow bell peppers, cut into 1-inch pieces
1 sweet potato, cut into 1-inch pieces
1 red onion, cut into wedges
3 tablespoons olive oil
2 teaspoons minced garlic
1 teaspoon chopped fresh thyme
Sea salt
Freshly ground black pepper

Preparation:

1. Line the air fryer basket with parchment paper and set aside. 2. In a large bowl, toss the olive oil, cauliflower, courgette, mushrooms, broccoli, bell peppers, sweet potato, onion, garlic, and thyme until well-mixed. Spread the vegetables in the air fryer basket and lightly season with the salt and pepper. 3. Roast at 200°C until the vegetables are tender and lightly caramelised, stirring occasionally, 20 to 25 minutes. 4. When done, serve and enjoy.
Per Serving: Calories 196; Fat 11g; Sodium 336mg; Carbs 22.7g; Fibre 4.8g; Sugar 6.77g; Protein 5.5g

Honey Glazed Carrots with Walnuts

⏰ **Prep: 5 minutes**　🍲 **Cook: 12 minutes**　❖ **Serves: 6**

Ingredients:
455g baby carrots
2 tablespoons olive oil
85g raw honey
¼ teaspoon ground cinnamon
30g black walnuts, chopped

Preparation:
1. In a large bowl, combine the baby carrots with the olive oil, honey, and cinnamon until well coated. 2. Pour into the air fryer basket and roast at 180°C for 6 minutes. Shake the basket, sprinkle the walnuts on top, and roast for 6 minutes more. 3. Remove the carrots from the air fryer and serve.
Per Serving: Calories 142; Fat 7.69g; Sodium 60mg; Carbs 18.47g; Fibre 2.6g; Sugar 15.26g; Protein 1.79g

Roasted Cauliflower Steaks with Baba Ghanoush

⏰ **Prep: 5 minutes**　🍲 **Cook: 25 minutes**　❖ **Serves: 4**

Ingredients:
85g small heads cauliflower
¼ teaspoon kosher or sea salt
¼ teaspoon smoked paprika
Extra-virgin olive oil, divided
1 container store-bought baba ghanoush

Preparation:
1. Stand one head of cauliflower on a cutting board, stem-end down. With a long chef's knife, slice down through the very centre of the head, including the stem. Starting at the cut edge, measure about 1 inch and cut one thick slice from each cauliflower half, including as much of the stem as possible, to make two cauliflower "steaks." Reserve the remaining cauliflower for another use. Repeat with the second cauliflower head. 2. Dry each steak well with a clean towel. Sprinkle the salt and smoked paprika evenly over both sides of each cauliflower steak. 3. In a large skillet, heat 2 tablespoons of oil over medium-high heat. When the oil is very hot, add two cauliflower steaks to the pan and cook for about 3 minutes, until golden and crispy. Flip and cook for 2 more minutes. Transfer the steaks to a plate. Use a pair of tongs to hold a paper towel and wipe out the pan to remove most of the hot oil (which will contain a few burnt bits of cauliflower). Repeat the cooking process with the remaining 2 tablespoons of oil and the remaining two steaks. 4. Put the cauliflower in the air fryer basket and roast at 200°C for 12 to 15 minutes until the cauliflower steaks are just fork tender; they will still be somewhat firm. 5. Serve the steaks with baba ghanoush.
Per Serving: Calories 72; Fat 1.14g; Sodium 188mg; Carbs 14.72g; Fibre 6.8g; Sugar 7.38g; Protein 3.91g

Roasted Brussels Sprouts Salad with Almonds

⏰ **Prep: 10 minutes**　🍲 **Cook: 35 minutes**　❖ **Serves: 4**

Ingredients:

For the Dressing:
60ml olive oil
80ml freshly squeezed lemon juice
2 tablespoons honey
1 teaspoon mustard
Sea salt
Freshly ground black pepper

For the Salad:
910g Brussels sprouts, trimmed and halved
2 tablespoons olive oil
1 teaspoon sea salt
65g baby spinach
10g baby arugula
1 shallot, halved and thinly sliced
3 tablespoons dried cranberries
60g blanched almonds, toasted
25g shredded halloumi cheese

Preparation:

To make the dressing: 1. In a small bowl, whisk together the honey, olive oil, lemon juice, and mustard. Season with the salt and pepper and set aside.

To make the salad: 1. Add the Brussels sprouts in a large mixing bowl, drizzle with the olive oil, and season with the salt. Toss to combine. 2. Spread the Brussels sprouts in the air fryer basket and roast at 220°C for 25 to 30 minutes, stirring once about halfway through, until crispy on the outside and tender on the inside. 3. While the Brussels sprouts are roasting, in a large mixing bowl, combine the spinach, shallot, arugula, cranberries, and almonds. Once cooked, add the roasted Brussels sprouts to the bowl. 4. Pour the dressing on the salad and toss to combine. Add shredded halloumi cheese and give it another gentle toss. Transfer the salad to a large serving platter. Serve.

Per Serving: Calories 463; Fat 31.91g; Sodium 1011mg; Carbs 40.28g; Fibre 11.8g; Sugar 19.07g; Protein 13.46g

Star Anise-Glazed Carrots

⏰ **Prep: 10 minutes**　🍲 **Cook: 15 minutes**　❖ **Serves: 4**

Ingredients:

4 large carrots, peeled and cut on the diagonal into 1-inch pieces
1 onion, thinly sliced
60ml extra-virgin olive oil
1 tablespoon balsamic vinegar
1 tablespoon lemon juice
2 teaspoons sugar or honey
1 teaspoon salt
1 teaspoon whole star anise, crushed slightly
¼ teaspoon freshly ground black pepper

Preparation:

1. Place the carrots, onion, balsamic vinegar, lemon juice, sugar, olive oil, salt, anise, and pepper in a medium bowl. Stir to make sure all the ingredients are evenly coated. 2. Pour the coated carrots into the air fryer basket and roast at 200°C about 15 to 20 minutes, stirring halfway through. Roast until the carrots are brown around the edges. 3. This is a make-ahead recipe, lasting at least 1 week tightly covered in the refrigerator or for several months in the freezer.

Per Serving: Calories 161; Fat 13.77g; Sodium 633mg; Carbs 9.67g; Fibre 2.2g; Sugar 5.43g; Protein 0.84g

Crispy Artichoke Hearts

⏰ **Prep: 10 minutes**   🍲 **Cook: 15 minutes**   📚 **Serves: 2**

Ingredients:

1 (425g) can artichoke hearts in water, drained
1 egg
1 tablespoon water
30g whole wheat bread crumbs
¼ teaspoon salt
¼ teaspoon paprika
½ lemon

Preparation:

1. In a medium shallow bowl, beat together the egg and water until frothy. 2. In a separate medium shallow bowl, mix together the bread crumbs, salt, and paprika. 3. Dip each artichoke heart into the egg mixture, then into the bread crumb mixture, coating the outside with the crumbs. Place the artichokes hearts in a single layer of the air fryer basket. 4. Fry the artichoke hearts at 195°C for 15 minutes. 5. Remove the artichokes from the air fryer, and squeeze the fresh lemon juice over the top before serving.

Per Serving: Calories 188; Fat 3.19g; Sodium 621mg; Carbs 33.22g; Fibre 12.2g; Sugar 3.36g; Protein 11.6g

Roasted Grape Tomatoes and Asparagus

⏰ **Prep: 5 minutes**   🍲 **Cook: 12 minutes**   📚 **Serves: 6**

Ingredients:

300g grape tomatoes
1 bunch asparagus, trimmed
2 tablespoons olive oil
3 garlic cloves, minced
½ teaspoon kosher salt

Preparation:

1. In a large bowl, combine all the ingredients, tossing until the vegetables are well coated with oil. 2. Pour the vegetable mixture into the air fryer basket in a single layer and roast at 195°C for 12 minutes. 3. When done, serve.

Per Serving: Calories 92; Fat 4.68g; Sodium 197mg; Carbs 12.54g; Fibre 2.1g; Sugar 9.23g; Protein 2.12g

Chapter 2 Vegetarian Mains

Lemon Tofu with Sun-Dried Tomatoes and Artichokes

⏱ Prep: 15 minutes 🍲 Cook: 30 minutes 🍽 Serves: 4

Ingredients:

1 (455g) package extra-firm tofu, drained and patted dry, cut into 1-inch cubes
2 tablespoons extra-virgin olive oil, divided
2 tablespoons lemon juice, divided
1 tablespoon low-sodium soy sauce or gluten-free tamari
1 onion, diced
½ teaspoon kosher salt
2 garlic cloves, minced
1 (395g) can artichoke hearts, drained
8 sun-dried tomato halves packed in oil, drained and chopped
¼ teaspoon freshly ground black pepper
1 tablespoon white wine vinegar
Zest of 1 lemon
15g fresh parsley, chopped

Preparation:

1. Line the air fryer basket with parchment paper or foil. 2. In a bowl, combine the tofu, 1 tablespoon of lemon juice, 1 tablespoon of olive oil, and soy sauce. Let sit and marinate for 15 to 30 minutes. Place the tofu in a single layer in the prepared basket and cook at 200°C for 20 minutes, turning once, until light golden brown. 3. In a large skillet or sauté pan over medium heat, heat the remaining 1 tablespoon olive oil. Add the onion and salt and sauté until translucent, 5 to 6 minutes. Add the garlic and sauté for 30 seconds. Add the sun-dried tomatoes, artichoke hearts, and black pepper and sauté for 5 minutes. Add the remaining 1 tablespoon of lemon juice and the white wine vinegar and deglaze the pan, scraping up any brown bits. Remove the pan from the heat and stir in the parsley and lemon zest. Gently mix in the cooked tofu. Serve.
Per Serving: Calories 316; Fat 20.21g; Sodium 540mg; Carbs 19.67g; Fibre 6.9g; Sugar 2.13g; Protein 21.35g

Roasted Tomato, Aubergine, and Chickpeas

⏱ Prep: 15 minutes 🍲 Cook: 60 minutes 🍽 Serves: 4

Ingredients:

Olive oil cooking spray
1 large (about 455g) aubergine, sliced into ¼-inch-thick rounds
1 teaspoon kosher salt, divided
1 tablespoon extra-virgin olive oil
3 garlic cloves, minced
1 (795g) can no-salt-added crushed tomatoes
½ teaspoon honey
¼ teaspoon freshly ground black pepper
2 tablespoons fresh basil, chopped
1 (425g) can no-salt-added or low-sodium chickpeas, drained and rinsed
85g crumbled feta cheese
1 tablespoon fresh oregano, chopped

Preparation:

1. Lightly spray the air fryer basket with the olive oil cooking spray. Arrange the aubergine in a single layer in the air fryer basket and sprinkle with ½ teaspoon of salt. Cook at 220°C for 20 minutes, until lightly golden brown, turning once halfway. 2. Meanwhile, in a large saucepan over medium heat, heat the olive oil. Add the garlic and sauté for 30 seconds. Add the honey, crushed tomatoes, the remaining ½ teaspoon salt, and black pepper. Simmer for about 20 minutes, until the sauce reduces a bit and thickens. Stir in the basil. 3. After removing the aubergine from the air fryer, reduce the temperature to 190°C. In a baking dish, ladle in the chickpeas and 250g sauce. Arrange the aubergine slices on top, overlapping as necessary to cover the chickpeas. Spread the remaining sauce over the aubergine. Sprinkle the feta cheese and oregano on top. 4. Cover the baking dish with foil and cook in the air fryer at 220°C for 15 minutes. Remove the foil and cook for an additional 15 minutes. 5. When done, serve and enjoy.
Per Serving: Calories 316; Fat 12.2g; Sodium 1039mg; Carbs 43.31g; Fibre 12.9g; Sugar 19.09g; Protein 14.09g

Parmesan and Thyme Roasted Butternut Squash

⏰ **Prep: 15 minutes** 🍲 **Cook: 20 minutes** 📚 **Serves: 4**

Ingredients:

590g butternut squash, cubed into 1-inch pieces (approximately 1 medium)
2 tablespoons olive oil
¼ teaspoon salt
¼ teaspoon garlic powder
¼ teaspoon black pepper
1 tablespoon fresh thyme
25g grated Parmesan

Preparation:

1. In a large bowl, combine the cubed squash with the olive oil, garlic powder, pepper, salt, and thyme until the squash is well coated. 2. Pour this mixture into the air fryer basket and roast at 180°C for 10 minutes. Stir and roast for an additional 8 to 10 minutes more. 3. Remove the squash from the air fryer and toss with the freshly grated Parmesan before serving.

Per Serving: Calories 127; Fat 8.59g; Sodium 262mg; Carbs 11.5g; Fibre 1.9g; Sugar 1.94g; Protein 2.74g

Crispy Aubergine Slices

⏰ **Prep: 5 minutes** 🍲 **Cook: 25 minutes** 📚 **Serves: 4**

Ingredients:

1 egg
1 tablespoon water
60g whole wheat bread crumbs
1 teaspoon garlic powder
½ teaspoon dried oregano
½ teaspoon salt
½ teaspoon paprika
1 medium aubergine, sliced into ¼-inch-thick rounds
1 tablespoon olive oil

Preparation:

1. In a medium shallow bowl, beat together the egg and water until frothy. 2. In a separate medium shallow bowl, mix together bread crumbs, oregano, salt, garlic powder, and paprika. 3. Dip each aubergine slice into the egg mixture, then into the bread crumb mixture, coating the outside with crumbs. Place the slices in a single layer at the bottom of the air fryer basket. 4. Drizzle the tops of the aubergine slices with the olive oil, then fry at 180°C for 15 minutes. Turn each slice and cook for an additional 10 minutes. 5. When done, serve and enjoy.

Per Serving: Calories 137; Fat 5.43g; Sodium 409mg; Carbs 18.66g; Fibre 4.9g; Sugar 5.77g; Protein 4.71g

Roasted Beets with Fresh Dill

⏱ **Prep: 10 minutes**   🍲 **Cook: 30 minutes**   ❖ **Serves: 4**

Ingredients:

4 beets, cleaned, peeled, and sliced
1 garlic clove, minced
2 tablespoons chopped fresh dill
¼ teaspoon salt
¼ teaspoon black pepper
3 tablespoons olive oil

Preparation:

1. In a large bowl, mix together all of the ingredients so the beets are well coated with the oil. 2. Pour the beet mixture into the air fryer basket and roast at 195°C for 15 minutes before stirring, then continue roasting for 15 minutes more. 3. When done, serve and enjoy.

Per Serving: Calories 136; Fat 10.75g; Sodium 210mg; Carbs 10.02g; Fibre 3.1g; Sugar 5.55g; Protein 1.91g

Roasted Broccoli Florets with Orange

⏱ **Prep: 5 minutes**   🍲 **Cook: 12 minutes**   ❖ **Serves: 6**

Ingredients:

350g broccoli florets (approximately 1 large head)
2 tablespoons olive oil
½ teaspoon salt
120ml orange juice
1 tablespoon raw honey
Orange wedges, for serving (optional)

Preparation:

1. In a large bowl, mix the broccoli, salt, orange juice, olive oil, and honey. Toss the broccoli in the liquid until well coated. 2. Pour the broccoli mixture into the air fryer basket and cook at 180°C for 6 minutes. Stir and cook for 6 minutes more. 3. Serve alone or with the orange wedges for additional citrus flavour, if desired.

Per Serving: Calories 81; Fat 4.75g; Sodium 214mg; Carbs 9.31g; Fibre 1.6g; Sugar 5.63g; Protein 1.86g

Chapter 2 Vegetarian Mains

Chapter 3 Snacks and Sides

Easy Air Fryer Popcorn	31
Greek Yoghurt Deviled Eggs	31
Goat Cheese Crostini with Basil	32
Air Fried Crab Cakes	32
Chinese Five-Spice Flavoured Popcorn	33
Crunchy Turmeric Roasted Chickpeas	33
Roasted Mini Potatoes	34
Crispy Pita Wedges	34
Tasty Moroccan Courgette Spread	35
Mashed Fava Beans Crostini	35
Lemon Cauliflower with Saffron Dipping Sauce	36
Healthy Trail Mix	36

Easy Air Fryer Popcorn

⏰ Prep: 2 minutes   🍱 Cook: 10 minutes   ❖ Serves: 2

Ingredients:

2 tablespoons olive oil
50g popcorn kernels
1 teaspoon garlic salt

Preparation:

1. Tear a square of aluminium foil the size of the bottom of the air fryer and place it into the air fryer. 2. Drizzle olive oil over the foil, and then pour in the popcorn kernels. 3. Roast at 195°C for 8 to 10 minutes or until the popcorn stops popping. 4. Transfer the popcorn to a large bowl and sprinkle with the garlic salt before serving.

Per Serving: Calories 125; Fat 13.55g; Sodium 1mg; Carbs 1.24g; Fibre 0.2g; Sugar 0.02g; Protein 0.22g

Greek Yoghurt Deviled Eggs

⏰ Prep: 10 minutes   🍱 Cook: 15 minutes   ❖ Serves: 4

Ingredients:

4 eggs
60g nonfat plain Greek yoghurt
1 teaspoon chopped fresh dill
⅛ teaspoon salt
⅛ teaspoon paprika
⅛ teaspoon garlic powder
Chopped fresh parsley, for garnish

Preparation:

1. Place the eggs in a single layer in the air fryer basket and cook at 125°C for 15 minutes. 2. Quickly remove the eggs from the air fryer and place them in a cold water bath. Let the eggs cool in the water for 10 minutes before removing and peeling them. 3. After peeling the eggs, cut them in half. 4. Spoon the yolk into a small bowl. Add the yoghurt, paprika, dill, salt, and garlic powder and mix until smooth. 5. Spoon or pipe the yolk mixture into the halved egg whites. Sprinkle the fresh parsley on top and serve. You can garnish with other herbs if desired.

Per Serving: Calories 75; Fat 4.42g; Sodium 151mg; Carbs 1.94g; Fibre 0.6g; Sugar 0.54g; Protein 6.85g

Goat Cheese Crostini with Basil

⏰ **Prep: 3 minutes**   🍱 **Cook: 5 minutes**   ❖ **Serves: 4**

Ingredients:

1 whole wheat baguette
60ml olive oil
2 garlic cloves, minced
115g goat cheese
2 tablespoons fresh basil, minced

Preparation:

1. Cut the baguette into ½-inch-thick slices. 2. In a small bowl, combine the olive oil with garlic, then brush it over one side of each slice of bread. 3. Place the olive-oil-coated bread in a single layer in the air fryer basket and bake at 195°C for 5 minutes. 4. Meanwhile, in a small bowl, mix together the goat cheese and basil. 5. Remove the toast from the air fryer, then spread a thin layer of the goat cheese mixture over the top of each piece and serve.
Per Serving: Calories 335; Fat 24.23g; Sodium 121mg; Carbs 19.14g; Fibre 2.7g; Sugar 0.74g; Protein 12.09g

Air Fried Crab Cakes

⏰ **Prep: 10 minutes**   🍱 **Cook: 10 minutes**   ❖ **Serves: 6**

Ingredients:

225g lump crab meat
2 tablespoons diced red bell pepper
1 scallion, white parts and green parts, diced
1 garlic clove, minced
1 tablespoon capers, minced
1 tablespoon nonfat plain Greek yoghurt
1 egg, beaten
30g whole wheat bread crumbs
¼ teaspoon salt
1 tablespoon olive oil
1 lemon, cut into wedges

Preparation:

1. In a medium bowl, mix the crab, scallion, garlic, bell pepper, and capers until combined. 2. Add the yoghurt and egg. Stir until incorporated. Mix in the bread crumbs and salt. 3. Divide this mixture into 6 equal portions and pat out into patties. Put the crab cakes into the air fryer basket in a single layer, making sure that they don't touch each other. Brush the tops of each patty with a bit of olive oil. 4. Cook at 180°C for 10 minutes. 5. Remove the crab cakes from the air fryer and serve with the lemon wedges on the side.
Per Serving: Calories 86; Fat 3.64g; Sodium 286mg; Carbs 4.34g; Fibre 0.3g; Sugar 0.7g; Protein 8.64g

Chinese Five-Spice Flavoured Popcorn

⏰ Prep: 5 minutes   🍲 Cook: 15 minutes   ❖ Serves: 8

Ingredients:

60g air-popped popcorn
2 tablespoons extra-virgin olive oil
2 tablespoons packed brown sugar
2 tablespoons Chinese five-spice powder
¼ teaspoon sea salt

Preparation:

1. Put the popcorn in a large bowl. Set aside. 2. In a small bowl, whisk the five-spice powder, olive oil, brown sugar, and sea salt. Pour the mixture over the popcorn, tossing to coat. Transfer the popcorn to the air fryer basket and cook at 175°C, stirring every 5 minutes or so, 15 minutes. 3. Serve hot or cool.

Per Serving: Calories 70; Fat 3.76g; Sodium 74mg; Carbs 8.45g; Fibre 1.2g; Sugar 2.06g; Protein 1.13g

Crunchy Turmeric Roasted Chickpeas

⏰ Prep: 15 minutes   🍲 Cook: 30 minutes   ❖ Serves: 4

Ingredients:

2 (425g) cans of organic chickpeas, drained and rinsed
3 tablespoons extra-virgin olive oil
2 teaspoons Turkish or smoked paprika
2 teaspoons turmeric
½ teaspoon dried oregano
½ teaspoon salt
¼ teaspoon ground ginger
⅛ teaspoon ground white pepper (optional)

Preparation:

1. Line the air fryer basket with parchment paper and set aside. 2. Completely dry the chickpeas. Lay the chickpeas out on a baking sheet, roll them around with paper towels, and allow them to air-dry. I usually let them dry for at least 2½ hours, but they can also be left to dry overnight. 3. In a medium bowl, combine the oregano, olive oil, salt, paprika, turmeric, ginger, and white pepper (if using). 4. Add the dry chickpeas to the bowl and toss to combine. 5. Place the chickpeas in the air fryer basket and cook at 200°C for 30 minutes or until the chickpeas turn golden brown. At 15 minutes, move the chickpeas around in the basket to avoid burning. Check every 10 minutes in case the chickpeas begin to crisp up before the full cooking time has elapsed. 6. Remove from the air fryer and set them aside to cool.

Per Serving: Calories 274; Fat 13.47g; Sodium 561mg; Carbs 30.99g; Fibre 8.8g; Sugar 5.33g; Protein 9.3g

Chapter 3 Snacks and Sides | 33

Roasted Mini Potatoes

⏰ **Prep: 30 minutes**　🍲 **Cook: 30 minutes**　🍃 **Serves: 2**

Ingredients:

285g golden mini potatoes, halved
4 tablespoons extra-virgin olive oil
2 teaspoons dried, minced garlic
1 teaspoon onion salt
½ teaspoon paprika
¼ teaspoon freshly ground black pepper
¼ teaspoon red pepper flakes
¼ teaspoon dried dill

Preparation:

1. Soak the potatoes and put them in a bowl of ice water for 30 minutes. Change the water if you return, and the water is milky. 2. Rinse and dry the potatoes, then put them on a baking sheet. 3. Drizzle the potatoes with oil and sprinkle with the garlic, onion salt, paprika, pepper, red pepper flakes, and dill. Using tongs or your hands, toss well to coat. 4. Put the potatoes in the air fryer basket and cook at 190°C for 20 minutes. 5. At 20 minutes, check and flip potatoes. Cook for another 10 minutes, or until the potatoes are fork-tender.
Per Serving: Calories 359; Fat 27.28g; Sodium 11mg; Carbs 27.13g; Fibre 3.6g; Sugar 1.59g; Protein 3.35g

Crispy Pita Wedges

⏰ **Prep: 10 minutes**　🍲 **Cook: 10-15 minutes**　🍃 **Serves: 6-8**

Ingredients:

1 (340g) package whole-wheat pita bread
60ml extra-virgin olive oil
1 teaspoon sea salt

Preparation:

1. Cut each pita bread into 12 wedges. 2. Place the pita wedges in a large bowl and drizzle with the olive oil and sea salt. 3. Arrange the pita in a single layer in the air fryer basket and toast the pita at 190°C until crisp and lightly browned, about 10 to 15 minutes. 4. The pita wedges can be stored in an airtight container at room temperature for about 10 days.
Per Serving: Calories 230; Fat 10.47g; Sodium 640mg; Carbs 31.19g; Fibre 4.2g; Sugar 0.46g; Protein 5.56g

Tasty Moroccan Courgette Spread

⏱ **Prep: 10 minutes**   🍳 **Cook: 20 minutes**   ⊛ **Serves: 4**

Ingredients:

60ml plus 1 tablespoon extra-virgin olive oil, divided, plus more for drizzling
4 large courgette, cut in half lengthwise
2 teaspoons salt, divided
60g tahini
1 garlic clove, minced
60ml lemon juice
½ teaspoon dried oregano
¼ teaspoon cayenne pepper
2 scallions, thinly sliced
1 tablespoon chopped fresh mint

Preparation:

1. Brush the air fryer basket with olive oil. 2. Brush the courgette with 60ml olive oil and sprinkle with 1 teaspoon salt. Place the courgette skin side down on the oiled basket. 3. Roast at 190°C for 15 to 20 minutes or until the courgette is so soft it can be mashed with a fork. 4. Place the courgette in a medium bowl and use a fork or potato masher to mash. 5. Mix in the tahini, 1 tablespoon olive oil, lemon juice, garlic, 1 teaspoon salt, oregano, and cayenne. 6. Add the scallions and mint and mix well. 7. Spoon the mixture into a serving bowl, drizzle with the olive oil, and serve warm or at room temperature. 8. The spread will keep 5 days in the refrigerator or in the freezer for several months.

Per Serving: Calories 218; Fat 21.82g; Sodium 1181mg; Carbs 5.13g; Fibre 1.7g; Sugar 0.48g; Protein 3.11g

Mashed Fava Beans Crostini

⏱ **Prep: 10 minutes**   🍳 **Cook: 10 minutes**   ⊛ **Serves: 4-6**

Ingredients:

1 whole-grain baguette, sliced into ¼-inch slices
60ml plus 80ml extra-virgin olive oil, divided
2 teaspoons salt, divided
1 (285g) package of frozen fava beans, thawed
1 garlic clove, smashed
60ml lemon juice
¼ teaspoon freshly ground black pepper
1 tablespoon chopped fresh mint

Preparation:

1. Lay the bread slices in the air fryer basket in a single layer. 2. Brush the bread with 60ml olive oil and sprinkle with 1 teaspoon salt. 3. Toast at 190°C for about 10 to 12 minutes or until lightly golden. Set aside. 4. Place the fava beans, garlic, 78ml olive oil, 1 teaspoon salt, lemon juice, and the pepper in a food processor or blender and process until smooth. The spread will have a coarse texture. 5. Add the chopped mint. Spread the fava bean mixture on the cooled crostini and serve. 6. The fava bean spread can be stored in the refrigerator for 4 days or frozen for several months.

Per Serving: Calories 369; Fat 14.89g; Sodium 1170mg; Carbs 46.73g; Fibre 14.5g; Sugar 3.17g; Protein 15.67g

Lemon Cauliflower with Saffron Dipping Sauce

⏰ **Prep: 10 minutes** 🍳 **Cook: 15 minutes** 🍽 **Serves: 4**

Ingredients:

For the Cauliflower:
60ml extra-virgin olive oil
2 teaspoons salt
1 teaspoon smoked hot paprika (or chipotle powder)
1 head cauliflower, stem trimmed, cut into florets
½ lemon

For the Saffron Sauce:
¼ teaspoon saffron threads
1 tablespoon water
245g Greek yoghurt
1 teaspoon salt
½ teaspoon ground turmeric
1 scallion, finely chopped
1 tablespoon chopped fresh cilantro

Preparation:

Make the cauliflower: 1. In a large bowl, mix the olive oil, salt, and paprika or chipotle powder. Add the cauliflower and mix well until it is evenly coated. 2. Place the cauliflower in a single layer in the air fryer basket. 3. Roast at 200°C until the cauliflower is brown around the edges, about 15 minutes, stirring occasionally. 4. Squeeze the lemon juice over the cauliflower.

Make the saffron sauce: 1. In a small bowl or saucer, combine the saffron threads with the water. This releases the colour and flavour. 2. In a small bowl, combine the salt, yoghurt, turmeric, saffron-water mixture, scallion, and cilantro. Mix well. 3. Arrange the cauliflower on a serving dish along with a bowl of saffron dip, and serve. 4. The cooked cauliflower will last 5 days in the refrigerator, and the sauce will last 4 days in the refrigerator.

Per Serving: Calories 178; Fat 15.78g; Sodium 1793mg; Carbs 7.16g; Fibre 1.6g; Sugar 4.34g; Protein 3.55g

Healthy Trail Mix

⏰ **Prep: 5 minutes** 🍳 **Cook: 30 minutes** 🍽 **Serves: 10-12**

Ingredients:

120g raw almonds
120g walnut halves
120g pumpkin seeds
130g dried apricots, cut into thin strips
120g dried cherries, roughly chopped
145g golden raisins
2 tablespoons extra-virgin olive oil
1 teaspoon salt

Preparation:

1. In a large bowl, mix the almonds, walnuts, pumpkin seeds, apricots, cherries, and raisins. Pour the olive oil over all and toss well with clean hands. Add salt and toss again to distribute. 2. Pour the nut mixture into the air fryer basket in a single layer and bake at 150°C until the fruits begin to brown, about 30 minutes. Cool in the basket to room temperature. 3. Store in a large airtight container or zipper-top plastic bag.

Per Serving: Calories 341; Fat 23.42g; Sodium 268mg; Carbs 29.87g; Fibre 5.2g; Sugar 19.65g; Protein 9.52g

Chapter 3 Snacks and Sides

Chapter 4 Pizza, Bread and Pasta

Perfect Mediterranean Veggie Pizza 38

Pesto Pita Pizza with Mushrooms 38

White Clam Pizza Pie 39

Chicken Artichoke Pizza with Olives 39

Greek Yoghurt Cornbread 40

Lamb Pita Pizza with Pine Nuts 40

Flavourful Lasagna with Three Sauces 41

Roasted Asparagus Caprese Pasta 41

No-Knead Sesame Bread 42

Sweet Anise Bread 42

Perfect Mediterranean Veggie Pizza

⏰ Prep: 15 minutes   🍳 Cook: 15 minutes   🍽 Serves: 4

Ingredients:

Nonstick cooking spray
3 tablespoons cornmeal
120g white whole-wheat flour or regular whole-wheat flour
65g all-purpose flour
1 tablespoon dried oregano, crushed between your fingers
¼ teaspoon kosher or sea salt
235ml plus 2 tablespoons 2% milk
2 large eggs, beaten
1 large bell pepper, sliced into ⅛-inch-thick rounds
1 (65g) can sliced olives, any type of green or black, drained
3 whole canned artichoke hearts, drained and quartered
20g thinly sliced red onion (about ⅙ onion)
55g feta cheese, crumbled
Extra-virgin olive oil, for topping (optional)

Preparation:

1. Spray a baking pan that fits your air fryer with nonstick cooking spray. Sprinkle it with the cornmeal and set aside. 2. In a large bowl, whisk together the flours, oregano, and salt. In a small bowl, stir together the milk and eggs; mix into the flour mixture until well combined. 3. Pour the mixture onto the prepared baking pan. Using a rubber scraper, carefully spread the batter evenly to the corners of the pan. Arrange the bell pepper slices evenly over the batter. 4. Place the baking pan into the air fryer and bake at 200°C for 10 to 12 minutes, or until the crust is dry on top. Remove the pizza crust from the air fryer. 5. Top the pizza crust with the olives, artichoke hearts, and onion. Top with the feta cheese. 6. Cook until the cheese is melted and golden, rotating the baking sheet halfway through and watching carefully to prevent burning. Top with a drizzle of olive oil.
Per Serving: Calories 382; Fat 10.86g; Sodium 615mg; Carbs 57.72g; Fibre 11.5g; Sugar 6.34g; Protein 18.27g

Pesto Pita Pizza with Mushrooms

⏰ Prep: 15 minutes   🍳 Cook: 10-15 minutes   🍽 Serves: 4

Ingredients:

60ml extra-virgin olive oil
12 large mushrooms, sliced
1 teaspoon salt
¼ teaspoon red pepper flakes (optional)
4 whole-wheat pita breads
115g Pesto
50g shredded Parmesan cheese

Preparation:

1. Warm a medium skillet over high heat, then add the olive oil, salt, mushrooms, and red pepper flakes (if using). Sauté until the liquid from the mushrooms has evaporated, about 5 to 7 minutes. 2. Place the pita breads on a baking pan. Spread the pesto over the pitas and top with the mushrooms and Parmesan cheese. 3. Place the baking pan into the air fryer and bake at 190°C for 10 to 15 minutes, or until the pizzas are lightly browned. 4. When done, serve immediately.
Per Serving: Calories 482; Fat 34.96g; Sodium 1214mg; Carbs 20.89g; Fibre 3.1g; Sugar 2g; Protein 11.51g

Chapter 4 Pizza, Bread and Pasta

White Clam Pizza Pie

⏰ Prep: 10 minutes   🍳 Cook: 20 minutes   🍽 Serves: 4

Ingredients:

455g refrigerated fresh pizza dough
Nonstick cooking spray
2 tablespoons extra-virgin olive oil, divided
2 garlic cloves, minced (about 1 teaspoon)
½ teaspoon crushed red pepper
1 (285g) can whole baby clams, drained, 180ml of juice reserved
60ml dry white wine
All-purpose flour, for dusting
115g diced fresh or shredded mozzarella cheese
1 tablespoon grated Pecorino Romano or Parmesan cheese
1 tablespoon chopped fresh flat-leaf (Italian) parsley

Preparation:

1. Take the pizza dough out of the refrigerator. Coat a baking pan with the nonstick cooking spray. 2. In a large skillet, heat 1½ tablespoons of the oil over medium heat. Add the garlic and crushed red pepper and cook for 1 minute, stirring frequently to prevent the garlic from burning. Add the reserved clam juice and wine. Bring to a boil over high heat. Reduce to medium heat so the sauce is just simmering and cook for 10 minutes, stirring occasionally. The sauce will cook down and thicken. 3. Stir in the clams and cook for 3 minutes, stirring occasionally. 4. While the sauce is cooking, on a lightly floured surface, form the pizza dough into a 12-inch circle or into a 10-by-12-inch rectangle with a rolling pin or by stretching with your hands. You can form the pizza dough into other size that fits your baking pan. Place the dough on the prepared baking pan. Brush the dough with the remaining ½ tablespoon of oil. Set aside until the clam sauce is ready. 5. Spread the clam sauce over the prepared dough within ½ inch of the edge. Top with the mozzarella cheese, then sprinkle with the Pecorino Romano. 6. Place the baking pan into the air fryer and bake at 200°C for 10 minutes, or until the crust starts to brown around the edges. 7. Remove the pizza from the air fryer and slide onto a wooden cutting board. Top with the parsley, use a pizza cutter or a sharp knife to cut into eight pieces, and serve.
Per Serving: Calories 439; Fat 18.26g; Sodium 1300mg; Carbs 43.95g; Fibre 2.8g; Sugar 6.5g; Protein 24.86g

Chicken Artichoke Pizza with Olives

⏰ Prep: 15 minutes   🍳 Cook: 10-15 minutes   🍽 Serves: 4

Ingredients:

1 (14- or 16-inch) cooked pizza crust (ideally thin crust)
1 tablespoon extra-virgin olive oil
225g Yoghurt Cheese
2 garlic cloves, thinly sliced
3 scallions, thinly sliced
290g diced cooked chicken
1 (395g) can artichoke hearts, drained, rinsed, cut in half
50g grated Parmesan cheese
60g pitted green olives

Preparation:

1. Place the pizza crust on a baking pan. Brush with the olive oil. 2. Top with an even layer of yoghurt cheese. 3. Arrange the garlic, scallions, artichoke hearts, chicken, Parmesan cheese, and olives over the top. 4. Place the baking pan into the air fryer and bake at 200°C for about 10 minutes or until the pizza is lightly browned. 5. Cooked pizza is best eaten right away. However, you can wrap leftovers in foil and refrigerate it for several days. Reheat in the air fryer or toaster oven for best results.
Per Serving: Calories 376; Fat 15.59g; Sodium 669mg; Carbs 24.75g; Fibre 3.7g; Sugar 4.9g; Protein 33.53g

Greek Yoghurt Cornbread

⏰ Prep: 15 minutes   🍲 Cook: 25 minutes   ♦ Serves: 4-6

Ingredients:

78ml olive oil, plus extra for greasing
125g cornmeal
125g all-purpose flour
50g sugar
½ teaspoon baking soda
½ teaspoon baking powder
1 teaspoon sea salt
245g plain full-fat Greek yoghurt
1 large egg
30g crumbled feta cheese

Preparation:

1. Lightly grease a square baking dish with the olive oil. 2. In a large bowl, stir together the cornmeal, flour, sugar, baking soda, baking powder, and salt until well mixed. Add the olive oil, yoghurt, and egg and stir until smooth. Stir in the feta. 3. Pour the batter into the prepared baking dish. Place the baking dish into the air fryer and bake at 190°C until a toothpick inserted into the centre of the corn bread comes out clean, about 30 minutes. 4. Remove the corn bread from the air fryer, cut it into 9 squares, and serve.

Per Serving: Calories 418; Fat 18.36g; Sodium 715mg; Carbs 53.08g; Fibre 1.9g; Sugar 9.26g; Protein 9.71g

Lamb Pita Pizza with Pine Nuts

⏰ Prep: 15 minutes   🍲 Cook: 25 minutes   ♦ Serves: 4

Ingredients:

1 tablespoon extra-virgin olive oil
1 small onion, chopped
1 garlic clove, chopped
455g ground lamb
1 teaspoon ground cumin
½ teaspoon ground cinnamon
120g tomato sauce
35g raisins
1 teaspoon salt
¼ teaspoon red pepper flakes (optional)
4 whole-wheat pita breads
30g toasted pine nuts (pignoli)
55g feta cheese, crumbled
15g chopped fresh flat leaf parsley

Preparation:

1. Place a large skillet over high heat. Add the olive oil, onion, and garlic, and sauté until the vegetables are soft, about 5 minutes. 2. Add the lamb and cook until all the pink is gone, about 5 minutes. 3. Add the cumin, tomato sauce, raisins, salt, cinnamon, and red pepper flakes (if using), and simmer an additional 5 minutes, or until most of the liquid in the tomato sauce has evaporated. 4. Place the pita breads on a baking pan and divide the lamb mixture among the four pita breads. Top each pita with the pine nuts, feta, and parsley. 5. Place the baking pan into the air fryer and bake at 190°C for about 10 minutes to heat through and toast the pita. Serve immediately. 6. The lamb filling can be made several days ahead. Keep in an airtight container in the refrigerator.

Per Serving: Calories 468; Fat 27.28g; Sodium 1366mg; Carbs 26.91g; Fibre 5.3g; Sugar 5.7g; Protein 30.58g

Flavourful Lasagna with Three Sauces

⏱ Prep: 30 minutes   🍳 Cook: 45 minutes   🍽 Serves: 8

Ingredients:

245g ricotta
130g Basil Pesto, or store-bought
970g Basic Tomato Basil Sauce, or store-bought, divided
2 (255g) packages no-boil lasagna sheets
335g Béchamel Sauce, divided
50g freshly grated Parmesan cheese

Preparation:

1. In a small mixing bowl, mix the ricotta and pesto. Set aside. 2. Spread 245g of tomato sauce on the bottom of a baking dish. Cover the sauce with a few lasagna sheets. 3. Spread 170g of béchamel sauce evenly on top of the lasagna sheets. Cover with a few more lasagna sheets. 4. Spread the ricotta and pesto mixture evenly over the lasagna sheets. 5. Pour 245g of tomato sauce over the ricotta layer and cover the sauce with a few lasagna sheets. 6. Spread the remaining 165g of béchamel sauce over the lasagna sheets. Cover with a few more lasagna sheets. 7. Pour the remaining 490 of tomato sauce over the sheets. Top with the Parmesan cheese. 8. Place the baking dish into the air fryer and bake at 190°C for 30 minutes or until the cheese on top is melted and golden brown. Let rest for 15 minutes before serving.

Per Serving: Calories 456; Fat 23.04g; Sodium 1499mg; Carbs 48.62g; Fibre 9g; Sugar 21.62g; Protein 21.47g

Roasted Asparagus Caprese Pasta

⏱ Prep: 10 minutes   🍳 Cook: 15 minutes   🍽 Serves: 6

Ingredients:

225g uncooked small pasta, like orecchiette (little ears) or farfalle (bow ties)
680g fresh asparagus, ends trimmed and stalks chopped into 1-inch pieces
310g grape tomatoes, halved
2 tablespoons extra-virgin olive oil
¼ teaspoon freshly ground black pepper
¼ teaspoon kosher or sea salt
225g fresh mozzarella, drained and cut into bite-size pieces
10g torn fresh basil leaves
2 tablespoons balsamic vinegar

Preparation:

1. In a large stockpot, cook the pasta according to the package directions. Drain, reserving about 60ml of the pasta water. 2. While the pasta is cooking, in a large bowl, toss the asparagus, oil, pepper, tomatoes, and salt together. Spread the mixture to the air fryer basket and cook at 200°C for 15 minutes, stirring twice as it cooks. 3. Remove the vegetables from the air fryer and transfer to a large bowl. Add the cooked pasta to the bowl. Mix with a few tablespoons of pasta water to help the sauce become smoother and the saucy vegetables stick to the pasta. 4. Gently mix in the mozzarella and basil. Drizzle with the balsamic vinegar. Serve and enjoy.

Per Serving: Calories 194; Fat 4.98g; Sodium 381mg; Carbs 24.08g; Fibre 5.2g; Sugar 9.33g; Protein 15.74g

No-Knead Sesame Bread

⏰ **Prep: 20 minutes**   🍲 **Cook: 10 minutes**   📚 **Serves: 8**

Ingredients:

3 tablespoons olive oil, divided
½ yield Pita Bread dough
30g all-purpose flour, for dusting
1 large egg yolk
60ml milk
1 tablespoon white sesame seeds
1 tablespoon black sesame seeds

Preparation:

1. Coat 2 baking sheets with 1 tablespoon of olive oil each and set aside. 2. Coat a large bowl with the remaining 1 tablespoon of olive oil. Place the dough in the bowl, cover with a clean kitchen towel, and allow to rise for 1 hour or until the dough doubles in size. 3. Dust a work surface with flour and turn the dough out on to it. Cut the dough into 2 balls. Keep dusting with flour to prevent sticking. Roll out the balls into ½-inch-thick flat circles. Place each dough circle on a prepared baking sheet. Cover and let rest for 30 minutes. 4. In a small bowl, whisk the egg yolk and milk until combined. Set aside. 5. Using your fingertips, dent the tops of the dough all over. Brush the dough with the egg-and-milk glaze. Sprinkle 1½ teaspoons each of white and black sesame seeds over each dough circle. 6. Working in batches, place the dough in the air fryer basket lined with parchment paper and bake at 230°C for about 10 minutes or until the edges begin to brown. Serve warm.

Per Serving: Calories 106; Fat 7.38g; Sodium 49mg; Carbs 8.03g; Fibre 0.9g; Sugar 0.49g; Protein 2.62g

Sweet Anise Bread

⏰ **Prep: 20 minutes**   🍲 **Cook: 60 minutes**   📚 **Serves: 8**

Ingredients:

2 tablespoons olive oil, plus more for preparing the pan
250g all-purpose flour, plus more for dusting
190g sugar
1½ teaspoons baking powder
1 teaspoon aniseed
½ teaspoon ground cinnamon
¼ teaspoon salt
1 large egg
120ml milk
1 tablespoon freshly squeezed orange juice
Grated zest of 1 orange

Preparation:

1. Coat a loaf pan with the olive oil. Set aside. 2. In a medium bowl, whisk the flour, aniseed, sugar, cinnamon, baking powder, and salt. Set aside. 3. In a small bowl, whisk the egg, olive oil, milk, orange juice, and orange zest. Add the egg mixture to the flour mixture and mix until well combined and a smooth dough forms. 4. Dust a work surface with the flour. Place the dough on it and flatten the dough to fit into the prepared loaf pan. Place the dough in the pan. 5. Place the pan into the air fryer and bake at 190°C for about 50 minutes or until golden. Let the bread rest in the pan for 10 minutes. Transfer to a wire rack to cool completely.

Per Serving: Calories 213; Fat 4.78g; Sodium 90mg; Carbs 37.95g; Fibre 1g; Sugar 13.27g; Protein 4.52g

Chapter 5 Fish and Seafood Mains

Provencal Salmon Fillets ………………………………… 44

Steamed Cod with Onions & Swiss Chard ……………… 44

Crispy Polenta Fish Sticks………………………………… 45

Salmon with Orange and Dill …………………………… 45

Garlic Shrimp and Mushroom Pasta …………………… 46

Foil Baked Fish with Garlic ……………………………… 46

Roasted Fish Fillets with Green Beans and Tomatoes ……… 47

Delicious Pollock Fillets with Roasted Tomatoes …………… 47

Roasted Halibut in Parchment with Courgette and Thyme 48

Honey Glazed Salmon Fillets …………………………… 48

Provencal Salmon Fillets

⏰ **Prep: 15 minutes**   🍳 **Cook: 25 minutes**   🍽 **Serves: 4**

Ingredients:

1 tablespoon olive oil
1 red bell pepper, chopped
½ sweet onion, chopped
2 teaspoons minced garlic
3 large tomatoes, chopped
65g shredded kale
60ml dry white wine
30g pitted, sliced black olives
2 tablespoons capers
1 teaspoon chopped fresh thyme
1 teaspoon chopped fresh parsley
4 (115g) salmon fillets

Preparation:

1. In a large ovenproof skillet over medium-high heat, heat the olive oil. Sauté the bell pepper, onion, and garlic until softened, about 4 minutes. 2. Add the tomatoes, kale, and wine and bring the mixture to a boil. Reduce the heat to low and simmer until the sauce thickens slightly, about 5 minutes. 3. Stir in the olives, thyme, capers, and parsley. Transfer the mixture in the skillet to a baking pan and nestle the salmon fillets in the sauce. 4. Place the baking pan into the air fryer and cook at 200°C until the fish flakes easily with a fork, 15 to 18 minutes. 5. Remove from the air fryer and serve the salmon topped with the sauce.
Per Serving: Calories 141; Fat 7.26g; Sodium 300mg; Carbs 11.17g; Fibre 2.8g; Sugar 6.42g; Protein 9.39g

Steamed Cod with Onions & Swiss Chard

⏰ **Prep: 5 minutes**   🍳 **Cook: 12 minutes**   🍽 **Serves: 4**

Ingredients:

1 teaspoon salt
½ teaspoon dried oregano
½ teaspoon dried thyme
½ teaspoon garlic powder
4 cod fillets
½ white onion, thinly sliced
70g Swiss chard, washed, stemmed, and torn into pieces
60ml olive oil
1 lemon, quartered

Preparation:

1. In a small bowl, whisk together the salt, thyme, oregano, and garlic powder. 2. Tear off four pieces of aluminium foil, with each sheet being large enough to envelop one cod fillet and a quarter of the vegetables. 3. Place a cod fillet in the middle of each sheet of foil, then sprinkle on all sides with the spice mixture. 4. In each foil packet, place a quarter of the onion slices and 20g Swiss chard, then drizzle 1 tablespoon olive oil and squeeze ¼ lemon over the contents of each foil packet. 5. Fold and seal the sides of the foil packets and then place them into the air fryer basket. Cook at 195°C for 12 minutes. 6. Remove from the air fryer, and carefully open each packet to avoid a steam burn.
Per Serving: Calories 213; Fat 14.07g; Sodium 972mg; Carbs 3.24g; Fibre 0.7g; Sugar 1.1g; Protein 18.32g

| Chapter 5 Fish and Seafood Mains

Crispy Polenta Fish Sticks

⏱ **Prep: 15 minutes**   🍳 **Cook: 10 minutes**   🍽 **Serves: 4**

Ingredients:

2 large eggs, lightly beaten 1 tablespoon 2% milk
455g skinned fish fillets (cod, tilapia, or other white fish) about ½ inch thick, sliced into 20 (1-inch-wide) strips
60g yellow cornmeal
60g whole-wheat panko bread crumbs or whole-wheat bread crumbs
¼ teaspoon smoked paprika
¼ teaspoon kosher or sea salt
¼ teaspoon freshly ground black pepper
Nonstick cooking spray

Preparation:

1. In a large bowl, mix the eggs and milk. Using a fork, add the fish strips to the egg mixture and stir gently to coat. 2. Put the cornmeal, bread crumbs, salt, smoked paprika, and pepper in a quart-size zip-top plastic bag. Using a fork or tongs, transfer the fish to the bag, letting the excess egg wash drip off into the bowl before transferring. Seal the bag and shake gently to fully coat each fish stick. 3. Spray a rimmed baking sheet with nonstick cooking spray. Using a fork or tongs, remove the fish sticks from the bag and arrange them in the air fryer basket, with space between them so the hot air can circulate and crisp them up. 4. Cook at 200°C for 5 to 8 minutes, until gentle pressure with a fork causes the fish to flake. 5. When done, serve and enjoy.

Per Serving: Calories 246; Fat 4.09g; Sodium 726mg; Carbs 26.25g; Fibre 1.6g; Sugar 1.29g; Protein 24.01g

Salmon with Orange and Dill

⏱ **Prep: 15 minutes**   🍳 **Cook: 15 minutes**   🍽 **Serves: 4**

Ingredients:

4 (170g) salmon fillets
2 tablespoons extra-virgin olive oil
½ teaspoon salt
¼ teaspoon freshly ground black pepper
Juice of large Valencia orange or tangerine
4 teaspoons orange or tangerine zest
4 tablespoons chopped fresh dill

Preparation:

1. Prepare four 10-inch-long pieces of aluminum foil. 2. Rub each salmon fillet on both sides with the olive oil. Season each with the salt and pepper and place one in the centre of each piece of foil. 3. Drizzle the orange juice over each piece of fish and top with 1 teaspoon orange zest and 1 tablespoon dill. 4. For each packet, fold the two long sides of the foil together and then fold the short ends in to make a packet. Make sure to leave about 2 inches of air space within the foil so the fish can steam. 5. Place the packets in the air fryer basket and cook at 190°C for 15 minutes. Open the packets carefully (they will be very steamy), transfer the fish to 4 serving plates, and pour the sauce over the top of each.

Per Serving: Calories 138; Fat 9.35g; Sodium 324mg; Carbs 8.1g; Fibre 2.4g; Sugar 3.06g; Protein 7.45g

Garlic Shrimp and Mushroom Pasta

⏰ **Prep: 10 minutes**　🍲 **Cook: 10 minutes**　🍽 **Serves: 6**

Ingredients:

455g small shrimp, peeled and deveined
60ml plus 1 tablespoon olive oil, divided
¼ teaspoon garlic powder
¼ teaspoon cayenne
455g whole grain pasta
5 garlic cloves, minced
225g baby bella mushrooms, sliced
50g Parmesan, plus more for serving (optional)
1 teaspoon salt
½ teaspoon black pepper
10g fresh basil

Preparation:

1. In a small bowl, add the shrimp, garlic powder, 1 tablespoon olive oil, and cayenne. Toss to coat the shrimp. 2. Place the shrimp into the air fryer basket and roast at 195°C for 5 minutes. Remove the shrimp and set aside. 3. Cook the pasta according to package directions. Once done cooking, reserve 60ml pasta water, then drain. 4. Meanwhile, in a large skillet, heat 60ml of olive oil over medium heat. Add the garlic and mushrooms and cook down for 5 minutes. 5. Pour the pasta, reserved pasta water, salt, Parmesan, pepper, and basil into the skillet with the vegetable-and-oil mixture and stir to coat the pasta. 6. Toss in the shrimp and remove from heat, then let the mixture sit for 5 minutes before serving with additional Parmesan, if desired.

Per Serving: Calories 184; Fat 3.44g; Sodium 749mg; Carbs 17.94g; Fibre 2.9g; Sugar 3.18g; Protein 21.86g

Foil Baked Fish with Garlic

⏰ **Prep: 10 minutes**　🍲 **Cook: 20 minutes**　🍽 **Serves: 4**

Ingredients:

4 (140g) cod or other white-fleshed fish fillets
2 to 3 tablespoons olive oil
2 to 3 garlic cloves, minced
1 tablespoon freshly squeezed lemon juice
Sea salt
Freshly ground black pepper

Preparation:

1. Cut four 12-inch squares of aluminium foil and lay them on a clean work surface. 2. Pat the fish dry with paper towels and place one fillet on each sheet of foil. 3. In a small bowl, mix the olive oil, garlic, and lemon juice and season with salt and pepper. Brush the oil mixture over both sides of the fish. Fold the foil over the fish to enclose it and crimp the edges of the foil to seal. 4. Place the foil packets in the air fryer basket and cook at 200°C for 15 to 20 minutes, until the fish is cooked through and flakes easily with a fork. 5. Remove the fish from the air fryer and serve. Be sure to tell your guests to be careful of the hot steam when opening their packets.

Per Serving: Calories 88; Fat 6.92g; Sodium 399mg; Carbs 0.95g; Fibre 0.1g; Sugar 0.11g; Protein 5.55g

Roasted Fish Fillets with Green Beans and Tomatoes

⏱ Prep: 10 minutes 🍳 Cook: 10 minutes 🍽 Serves: 4

Ingredients:

Nonstick cooking spray
2 tablespoons extra-virgin olive oil
1 tablespoon balsamic vinegar
4 (115g) fish fillets, such as cod or tilapia (½ inch thick)
340g green beans
310g cherry or grape tomatoes

Preparation:

1. Coat two baking pans with nonstick cooking spray. 2. In a small bowl, whisk together the oil and vinegar. Set aside. 3. Place two pieces of fish on each baking pan. 4. In a large bowl, combine the beans and tomatoes. Pour in the oil and vinegar, and toss gently to coat. Pour half of the green bean mixture over the fish on one baking pan, and the remaining half over the fish on the other. Turn the fish over, and rub it in the oil mixture to coat. Spread the vegetables evenly on the baking pans so hot air can circulate around them. 5. Working in batches, place the baking pan into the air fryer and cook at 200°C for 5 to 8 minutes, until the fish is just opaque and not translucent. The fish is done and ready to serve when it just begins to separate into flakes (chunks) when pressed gently with a fork.

Per Serving: Calories 146; Fat 7.2g; Sodium 91mg; Carbs 16.1g; Fibre 3.1g; Sugar 11.48g; Protein 6.22g

Delicious Pollock Fillets with Roasted Tomatoes

⏱ Prep: 5 minutes 🍳 Cook: 40 minutes 🍽 Serves: 6

Ingredients:

12 plum tomatoes, halved
2 shallots, very thinly cut into rings
3 garlic cloves, minced
3 tablespoons plus 1 teaspoon extra-virgin olive oil, divided
1 teaspoon sea salt, divided
½ teaspoon freshly ground black pepper, divided
1 teaspoon butter (or extra-virgin olive oil)
90g whole-wheat bread crumbs
6 (115g) pollock fillets
15g chopped fresh Italian parsley leaves

Preparation:

1. In a large bowl, toss the shallots, tomatoes, garlic, ½ teaspoon of sea salt, 1 tablespoon of olive oil, and ¼ teaspoon of pepper. 2. Arrange the tomatoes in a single layer in the air fryer basket and cook at 230°C for about 40 minutes until the tomatoes are soft and browned. 3. While the tomatoes cook, in a large nonstick skillet over medium-high heat, heat 1 tablespoon plus 1 teaspoon of olive oil until it bubbles. 4. Add the bread crumbs and cook for about 5 minutes, stirring, until they are browned and crunchy. Remove from the skillet and set aside, scraping the skillet clean. 5. Return the skillet to medium-high heat and add the remaining tablespoon of olive oil. 6. Season the fish with the remaining ½ teaspoon of sea salt and ¼ teaspoon of pepper. Place the fish in the skillet. Cook for about 5 minutes per side until opaque. 7. To assemble, spoon the tomatoes onto four plates. Top with the pollock and sprinkle with the bread crumbs. Garnish with the parsley and serve.

Per Serving: Calories 187; Fat 8.82g; Sodium 782mg; Carbs 14.71g; Fibre 1.8g; Sugar 0.88g; Protein 12.78g

Roasted Halibut in Parchment with Courgette and Thyme

Prep: 15 minutes **Cook: 15 minutes** **Serves: 4**

Ingredients:

60g courgette, diced
1 shallot, minced
4 (140g) halibut fillets (about 1 inch thick)
4 teaspoons extra-virgin olive oil
¼ teaspoon kosher salt
⅛ teaspoon freshly ground black pepper
1 lemon, sliced into ⅛-inch-thick rounds
8 sprigs of thyme

Preparation:

1. Combine the courgette and shallots in a medium bowl. 2. Cut 4 (15-by-24-inch) pieces of parchment paper. Fold each sheet in half horizontally. Draw a large half heart on one side of each folded sheet, with the fold along the centre of the heart. Cut out the heart, open the parchment, and lay it flat. 3. Place a fillet near the centre of each parchment heart. Drizzle 1 teaspoon olive oil on each fillet. Sprinkle with the salt and pepper. Top each fillet with the lemon slices and 2 sprigs of thyme. Sprinkle each fillet with one-quarter of the courgette and shallot mixture. Fold the parchment over. 4. Starting at the top, fold the edges of the parchment over and continue all the way around to make a packet. Twist the end tightly to secure it. 5. Arrange the 4 packets in the air fryer basket and cook at 230°C for about 15 minutes. 6. Place on plates; cut open. Serve immediately.

Per Serving: Calories 82; Fat 5.13g; Sodium 172mg; Carbs 2.25g; Fibre 0.6g; Sugar 1.08g; Protein 7.1g

Honey Glazed Salmon Fillets

Prep: 5 minutes **Cook: 12 minutes** **Serves: 4**

Ingredients:

85g raw honey
4 garlic cloves, minced
1 tablespoon olive oil
½ teaspoon salt
Olive oil cooking spray
4 (1½-inch-thick) salmon fillets

Preparation:

1. In a small bowl, mix together the honey, olive oil, garlic, and salt. 2. Spray the bottom of the air fryer basket with the olive oil cooking spray and place the salmon in a single layer on the bottom of the air fryer basket. 3. Brush the top of each fillet with the honey-garlic mixture, and roast at 195°C for 10 to 12 minutes or until the internal temperature reaches 60°C.

Per Serving: Calories 150; Fat 5.05g; Sodium 313mg; Carbs 18.48g; Fibre 0.1g; Sugar 17.44g; Protein 8.82g

Chapter 6 Poultry Mains

Crispy Breaded Turkey Cutlets 50

Crispy Chicken Tenders 50

Sumac Roasted Chicken with Cauliflower and Carrots 51

Herb Roasted Whole Chicken 51

Rosemary Roasted Chicken Drumsticks 52

Mediterranean Chicken Thighs 52

Classic Chicken Kebab with Vegetables 53

Air Fried Turkey Meatballs 53

Lemon Garlic Chicken Thighs 54

Chicken Kebabs with Tzatziki Sauce 54

Crispy Breaded Turkey Cutlets

⏰ **Prep: 5 minutes**   🍲 **Cook: 8 minutes**   ♦ **Serves: 4**

Ingredients:

60g whole wheat bread crumbs
¼ teaspoon paprika
¼ teaspoon salt
¼ teaspoon black pepper
⅛ teaspoon dried sage
⅛ teaspoon garlic powder
1 egg
4 turkey breast cutlets
Chopped fresh parsley for serving

Preparation:

1. In a medium shallow bowl, stir together the bread crumbs, paprika, black pepper, sage, salt, and garlic powder. 2. In a separate medium shallow bowl, whisk the egg until frothy. 3. Dip each turkey cutlet into the egg mixture, then into the bread crumb mixture, coating the outside with the crumbs. Place the breaded turkey cutlets in a single layer at the bottom of the air fryer basket, making sure that they don't touch each other. 4. Cook at 195°C for 4 minutes. Turn the cutlets over, then fry for 4 minutes more or until the internal temperature reaches 75°C. Sprinkle on the parsley and serve.
Per Serving: Calories 328; Fat 5.18g; Sodium 518mg; Carbs 11.34g; Fibre 1.2g; Sugar 1.14g; Protein 56.01g

Crispy Chicken Tenders

⏰ **Prep: 5 minutes**   🍲 **Cook: 12 minutes**   ♦ **Serves: 4**

Ingredients:

1 egg
60ml unsweetened almond milk
30g whole wheat flour
30g whole wheat bread crumbs
½ teaspoon salt
½ teaspoon black pepper
½ teaspoon dried thyme
½ teaspoon dried sage
½ teaspoon garlic powder
455g chicken tenderloins
1 lemon, quartered

Preparation:

1. In a shallow bowl, beat the egg and almond milk until frothy. 2. In a separate shallow bowl, stir together the flour, salt, bread crumbs, pepper, thyme, sage, and garlic powder. 3. Dip each chicken tenderloin into the egg mixture, then into the bread crumb mixture, coating the outside with the crumbs. Place the breaded chicken tenderloins into the bottom of the air fryer basket in an even layer, making sure that they don't touch each other. 4. Cook in the air fryer at 180°C for 6 minutes, then turn and cook for an additional 5 to 6 minutes. Serve with the lemon slices.
Per Serving: Calories 207; Fat 4.91g; Sodium 452mg; Carbs 13.24g; Fibre 1.4g; Sugar 2.12g; Protein 26.59g

Sumac Roasted Chicken with Cauliflower and Carrots

⏱ **Prep: 15 minutes**   🍲 **Cook: 40 minutes**   ❖ **Serves: 4**

Ingredients:

3 tablespoons extra-virgin olive oil
1 tablespoon ground sumac
1 teaspoon kosher salt
½ teaspoon ground cumin
¼ teaspoon freshly ground black pepper
685g bone-in chicken thighs and drumsticks
1 medium cauliflower, cut into 1-inch florets
2 carrots, peeled and cut into 1-inch rounds
1 lemon, cut into ¼-inch-thick slices
1 tablespoon lemon juice
15g fresh parsley, chopped
15g fresh mint, chopped

Preparation:

1. Line the air fryer basket with parchment paper or foil. 2. In a large bowl, stir together the olive oil, salt, cumin, sumac, and black pepper. Add the chicken, cauliflower, and carrots and toss until thoroughly coated with the oil and spice mixture. 3. Arrange the cauliflower, carrots, and chicken in a single layer in the prepared basket. Top with the lemon slices. 4. Roast at 220°C for 40 minutes, tossing the vegetables once halfway through. 5. Sprinkle the lemon juice over the chicken and vegetables and garnish with the parsley and mint.

Per Serving: Calories 494; Fat 45.85g; Sodium 690mg; Carbs 12.42g; Fibre 4g; Sugar 4.69g; Protein 10.94g

Herb Roasted Whole Chicken

⏱ **Prep: 15 minutes**   🍲 **Cook: 50-60 minutes**   ❖ **Serves: 6**

Ingredients:

1 (1,365 to 1,595g) roasting chicken
1 tablespoon extra-virgin olive oil
4 rosemary sprigs
6 thyme sprigs
4 fresh sage leaves
1 bay leaf
1 teaspoon freshly squeezed lemon juice
1 teaspoon salt
½ teaspoon freshly ground black pepper

Preparation:

1. Rub the olive oil all over the chicken. As you do, gently loosen the skin over the breast to form a pocket. 2. Slide half of the rosemary and thyme sprigs underneath the skin over the breast, and put the sage leaves, bay leaf, and remaining sprigs inside the cavity. 3. Rub with the lemon juice and season with salt and pepper. 4. Put the chicken in the air fryer basket and roast at 200°C until an instant-read thermometer inserted into the thigh registers 75°C, 50 to 60 minutes. 5. Remove from the air fryer and let rest for 10 minutes before carving.

Per Serving: Calories 276; Fat 8.49g; Sodium 558mg; Carbs 0.87g; Fibre 0.5g; Sugar 0.03g; Protein 46.25g

Rosemary Roasted Chicken Drumsticks

⏱ **Prep: 5 minutes**   🍲 **Cook: 60 minutes**   ≽ **Serves: 6**

Ingredients:

2 tablespoons chopped fresh rosemary leaves
1 teaspoon garlic powder
½ teaspoon sea salt
⅛ teaspoon freshly ground black pepper
Zest of 1 lemon
12 chicken drumsticks

Preparation:

1. In a small bowl, mix the rosemary, pepper, garlic powder, sea salt, and lemon zest. 2. Put the drumsticks in the air fryer basket and sprinkle with the rosemary mixture. 3. Cook at 175°C for about 1 hour or until the chicken reaches an internal temperature of 75°C.
Per Serving: Calories 423; Fat 23.98g; Sodium 470mg; Carbs 1.37g; Fibre 0.2g; Sugar 0.21g; Protein 47.15g

Mediterranean Chicken Thighs

⏱ **Prep: 5 minutes**   🍲 **Cook: 30-35 minutes**   ≽ **Serves: 6**

Ingredients:

2 tablespoons extra-virgin olive oil
2 teaspoons dried rosemary
1½ teaspoons ground cumin
1½ teaspoons ground coriander
¾ teaspoon dried oregano
⅛ teaspoon salt
6 bone-in, skin-on chicken thighs (about 3 pounds)

Preparation:

1. Line the air fryer basket with parchment paper. 2. Add the olive oil and spices into a large bowl and mix together, making a paste. Add the chicken and mix together until evenly coated. 3. Place the coated chicken in the air fryer basket and cook at 230°C for 30 to 35 minutes, or until golden brown and the chicken registers an internal temperature of 75°C.
Per Serving: Calories 427; Fat 33.52g; Sodium 194mg; Carbs 0.81g; Fibre 0.1g; Sugar 0.02g; Protein 28.84g

Classic Chicken Kebab with Vegetables

⏰ **Prep: 30 minutes**　🍳 **Cook: 25 minutes**　📚 **Serves: 4**

Ingredients:

60ml olive oil
1 teaspoon garlic powder
1 teaspoon onion powder
1 teaspoon ground cumin
½ teaspoon dried oregano
½ teaspoon dried basil
60ml lemon juice
1 tablespoon apple cider vinegar
Olive oil cooking spray
455g boneless skinless chicken thighs, cut into 1-inch pieces
1 red bell pepper, cut into 1-inch pieces
1 red onion, cut into 1-inch pieces
1 courgette, cut into 1-inch pieces
12 cherry tomatoes

Preparation:

1. In a large bowl, mix together the olive oil, onion powder, cumin, oregano, basil, garlic powder, lemon juice, and apple cider vinegar. 2. Spray six skewers with olive oil cooking spray. 3. On each skewer, slide on a piece of chicken, then a piece of bell pepper, onion, courgette, and finally a tomato and then repeat. Each skewer should have at least two pieces of each item. 4. Once all of the skewers are prepared, place them in a baking dish and pour the olive oil marinade over the top of the skewers. Turn each skewer so that all sides of the chicken and vegetables are coated. 5. Cover the dish with plastic wrap and place it in the refrigerator for 30 minutes. 6. Remove the skewers from the marinade and lay them in a single layer in the air fryer basket. 7. Cook at 195°C for 10 minutes. Rotate the kebabs, then cook them for 15 minutes more. 8. Remove the skewers from the air fryer and let them rest for 5 minutes before serving.

Per Serving: Calories 300; Fat 17.04g; Sodium 62mg; Carbs 9.57g; Fibre 2.1g; Sugar 4.8g; Protein 27.44g

Air Fried Turkey Meatballs

⏰ **Prep: 5 minutes**　🍳 **Cook: 12 minutes**　📚 **Serves: 4**

Ingredients:

455g ground turkey
1 egg
¼ teaspoon red pepper flakes
30g whole wheat bread crumbs
1 teaspoon salt
½ teaspoon garlic powder
½ teaspoon onion powder
½ teaspoon black pepper

Preparation:

1. In a large bowl, combine all ingredients and mix well. 2. Divide the meatball mixture into 12 portions. Roll each portion into a ball and place the balls into the bottom of the air fryer basket, making sure that they don't touch each other. 3. Cook at 180°C for 10 to 12 minutes or until the meatballs are cooked through and browned.

Per Serving: Calories 215; Fat 10.11g; Sodium 713mg; Carbs 5.97g; Fibre 0.5g; Sugar 0.64g; Protein 24.77g

Lemon Garlic Chicken Thighs

⏰ **Prep: 5 minutes**   🍲 **Cook: 22 minutes**   🍽 **Serves: 4**

Ingredients:

4 bone-in chicken thighs, skin and fat removed
2 tablespoons olive oil
1 teaspoon garlic powder
1 teaspoon salt
Black pepper
1 lemon, sliced

Preparation:

1. Coat the chicken thighs in the olive oil, garlic powder, and salt. 2. Tear off four pieces of aluminum foil, with each sheet being large enough to envelop one chicken thigh. 3. Place one chicken thigh on each piece of foil, season it with black pepper, and then top it with slices of lemon. 4. Place the foil packets into the air fryer basket and cook at 195°C for 20 to 22 minutes, or until the internal temperature of the chicken has reached 75°C. 5. Remove the foil packets from the air fryer. Carefully open each packet to avoid a steam burn.
Per Serving: Calories 299; Fat 14.75g; Sodium 766mg; Carbs 1.58g; Fibre 0.2g; Sugar 0.32g; Protein 38.15g

Chicken Kebabs with Tzatziki Sauce

⏰ **Prep: 45 minutes**   🍲 **Cook: 20 minutes**   🍽 **Serves: 4**

Ingredients:

120ml extra-virgin olive oil, divided
½ large lemon, juiced
2 garlic cloves, minced
½ teaspoon za'atar seasoning
Salt
Freshly ground black pepper
455g boneless skinless chicken breasts, cut into 1¼-inch cubes
1 large red bell pepper, cut into 1¼-inch pieces
2 small courgettes (nearly 1 pound), cut into rounds slightly under ½ inch thick
2 large shallots, diced into quarters
Tzatziki Sauce

Preparation:

1. In a bowl, whisk together 78ml of olive oil, garlic, za'atar, salt, lemon juice, and pepper. 2. Put the chicken in a medium bowl and pour the olive oil mixture over the chicken. Press the chicken into the marinade. Cover and refrigerate for 45 minutes. While the chicken marinates, soak the wooden skewers in water for 30 minutes. 3. Drizzle and toss the pepper, courgette, and shallots with the remaining 2½ tablespoons of olive oil and season lightly with the salt. 4. On each skewer, thread a red bell pepper, courgette, shallot and 2 chicken pieces and repeat twice. Put the kebabs in the air fryer basket. 5. Cook at 200°C for 7 to 9 minutes or until the chicken is cooked through. Rotate once halfway through cooking. 6. Serve the kebabs warm with the Tzatziki Sauce.
Per Serving: Calories 386; Fat 30.05g; Sodium 369mg; Carbs 2.54g; Fibre 0.4g; Sugar 0.78g; Protein 26.05g

| Chapter 6 Poultry Mains

Chapter 7 Red Meat Mains

Roasted Beef Tips with Yellow Onions 56

Greek Beef Meatloaf 56

Roasted Pork Tenderloin and Lemony Orzo 57

Simple Lamb Meatballs 57

Pork Roast with Apple Dijon Sauce 58

Sriracha Lamb Chops 58

Herbed Dijon Roasted Pork Tenderloin 59

Mini Greek Meatloaves 59

Authentic Greek Moussaka 60

Homemade Greek Meatballs (Keftedes) 60

Roasted Beef Tips with Yellow Onions

⏱ **Prep: 5 minutes**　　🍲 **Cook: 10 minutes**　　📚 **Serves: 4**

Ingredients:

455g rib eye steak, cubed
2 garlic cloves, minced
2 tablespoons olive oil
1 tablespoon fresh oregano
1 teaspoon salt
½ teaspoon black pepper
1 yellow onion, thinly sliced

Preparation:

1. In a medium bowl, combine the steak, oregano, salt, garlic, olive oil, pepper, and onion. Mix until all of the beef and onion are well coated. 2. Put the seasoned steak mixture into the air fryer basket. Roast at 195°C for 5 minutes. Stir and roast for 5 minutes more. 3. Let rest for 5 minutes before serving with some favourite sides.
Per Serving: Calories 258; Fat 16.45g; Sodium 647mg; Carbs 3.48g; Fibre 0.7g; Sugar 1.19g; Protein 24.77g

Greek Beef Meatloaf

⏱ **Prep: 5 minutes**　　🍲 **Cook: 25 minutes**　　📚 **Serves: 6**

Ingredients:

455g lean ground beef
2 eggs
2 Roma tomatoes, diced
½ white onion, diced
60g whole wheat bread crumbs
1 teaspoon garlic powder
1 teaspoon dried oregano
1 teaspoon dried thyme
1 teaspoon salt
1 teaspoon black pepper
55g mozzarella cheese, shredded
1 tablespoon olive oil
Fresh chopped parsley, for garnish

Preparation:

1. In a large bowl, mix together the ground beef, onion, bread crumbs, garlic powder, oregano, thyme, salt, eggs, tomatoes, pepper, and cheese. 2. Form into a loaf, flattening to 1-inch thick. 3. Brush the top with olive oil, then place the meatloaf into the air fryer basket and cook at 195°C for 25 minutes. 4. Remove from the air fryer and let rest for 5 minutes. Slice, garnish with the parsley, and serve.
Per Serving: Calories 208; Fat 8.64g; Sodium 618mg; Carbs 10.83g; Fibre 1.8g; Sugar 2.33g; Protein 22.47g

Roasted Pork Tenderloin and Lemony Orzo

⏲ **Prep: 15 minutes**   🍲 **Cook: 20 minutes**   ❖ **Serves: 6**

Ingredients:

455g pork tenderloin
½ teaspoon Shawarma Spice Rub
1 tablespoon salt
½ teaspoon coarsely ground black pepper
½ teaspoon garlic powder
6 tablespoons extra-virgin olive oil
335g Lemony Orzo

Preparation:

1. Rub the pork with shawarma seasoning, pepper, salt, and garlic powder and drizzle with the olive oil. 2. Put the pork into the air fryer basket and roast at 175°C for 20 minutes or until desired doneness. 3. Remove the pork from the air fryer and let it rest for 10 minutes. 4. Assemble the pork on a plate with the orzo and enjoy.
Per Serving: Calories 290; Fat 15.55g; Sodium 1367mg; Carbs 18.92g; Fibre 2.1g; Sugar 0.58g; Protein 19.63g

Simple Lamb Meatballs

⏲ **Prep: 15 minutes**   🍲 **Cook: 15 minutes**   ❖ **Serves: 4**

Ingredients:

455g ground lamb
3 scallions, thinly sliced
2 garlic cloves, minced
3 tablespoons rice flour
1 egg
1 teaspoon dried oregano
1 teaspoon salt
½ teaspoon ground cumin
¼ teaspoon red pepper flakes (optional)
¼ teaspoon freshly ground black pepper
Oil to coat the baking sheet

Preparation:

1. Place the ground lamb, scallions, egg, oregano, salt, cumin, garlic, rice flour, red pepper flakes (if using), and pepper in a medium bowl and mix well. 2. Oil a rimmed baking sheet. Using a 30g ice cream scoop, scoop the meatballs and place them on the oiled baking sheet. Leave about 1 inch around each meatball on the sheet so they brown nicely. 3. Transfer the meatballs to the air fryer basket and cook at 200°C for 12 to 15 minutes or until the meatballs are firm. 4. Arrange on a platter and serve. 5. These meatballs can be stored in the refrigerator for 1 week or frozen for several months.
Per Serving: Calories 370; Fat 28.04g; Sodium 665mg; Carbs 7.18g; Fibre 0.4g; Sugar 0.23g; Protein 20.84g

Pork Roast with Apple Dijon Sauce

⏰ **Prep: 15 minutes**   🍲 **Cook: 40 minutes**   ❖ **Serves: 4**

🌙 **Ingredients:**

1½ tablespoons extra-virgin olive oil
1 (340g) pork tenderloin
¼ teaspoon kosher salt
¼ teaspoon freshly ground black pepper
80g apple jelly
60ml apple juice
2 to 3 tablespoons Dijon mustard
½ tablespoon cornstarch
½ tablespoon cream

🌙 **Preparation:**

1. In a large sauté pan or skillet, heat the olive oil over medium heat. 2. Add the pork to the skillet, using tongs to turn and sear the pork on all sides. Once seared, sprinkle pork with salt and pepper and set it on a small baking sheet. 3. In the same skillet, with the juices from the pork, mix the apple jelly, juice, and mustard into the pan juices. Heat thoroughly over low heat, stirring consistently for 5 minutes. Spoon over the pork. 4. Put the pork in the air fryer basket and roast at 160°C for 15 to 17 minutes or 20 minutes per pound. Every 10 to 15 minutes, baste the pork with the apple-mustard sauce. 5. When the pork tenderloin is done, remove it from the air fryer and let it rest for 15 minutes. Then, cut it into 1-inch slices. 6. In a small pot, blend the cornstarch with cream. Heat over low heat. Add the pan juices into the pot, stirring for 2 minutes, until thickened. Serve the sauce over the pork.

Per Serving: Calories 168; Fat 7.75g; Sodium 321mg; Carbs 5.67g; Fibre 0.8g; Sugar 3.56g; Protein 18.36g

Sriracha Lamb Chops

⏰ **Prep: 2 minutes**   🍲 **Cook: 10 minutes**   ❖ **Serves: 4**

🌙 **Ingredients:**

4 (115g) loin lamb chops with bones, trimmed
Sea salt
Freshly ground black pepper
1 tablespoon olive oil
2 tablespoons Sriracha sauce
1 tablespoon chopped fresh cilantro

🌙 **Preparation:**

1. Lightly season the lamb chops with the salt and pepper. 2. In a large ovenproof skillet over medium-high heat, heat the olive oil. Brown the chops on both sides, about 2 minutes per side, and spread the chops with sriracha. 3. Transfer the chops to the air fryer and roast at 230°C until the desired doneness, 4 to 5 minutes for medium. 4. When done, serve topped with cilantro.

Per Serving: Calories 194; Fat 11.2g; Sodium 442mg; Carbs 0.81g; Fibre 0.2g; Sugar 0.36g; Protein 22.83g

Herbed Dijon Roasted Pork Tenderloin

⏲ **Prep: 10 minutes** 🍳 **Cook: 20 minutes** 🍽 **Serves: 6**

Ingredients:

30g fresh Italian parsley leaves, chopped
3 tablespoons fresh rosemary leaves, chopped
3 tablespoons fresh thyme leaves, chopped
3 tablespoons Dijon mustard
1 tablespoon extra-virgin olive oil
4 garlic cloves, minced
½ teaspoon sea salt
¼ teaspoon freshly ground black pepper
1 (685g) pork tenderloin

Preparation:

1. In a blender or food processor, combine the parsley, mustard, olive oil, garlic, sea salt, rosemary, thyme, and pepper. Process for about 30 seconds until smooth. Spread the mixture evenly over the pork. 2. Place the coated pork in the air fryer basket and cook at 200°C for about 20 minutes or until the meat reaches an internal temperature of 60°C. 3. Remove from the air fryer and let rest for 10 minutes. Slice and serve.

Per Serving: Calories 156; Fat 5.09g; Sodium 343mg; Carbs 1.98g; Fibre 0.8g; Sugar 0.13g; Protein 24.43g

Mini Greek Meatloaves

⏲ **Prep: 5 minutes** 🍳 **Cook: 25 minutes** 🍽 **Serves: 6**

Ingredients:

Nonstick cooking spray
1 tablespoon extra-virgin olive oil
96g minced onion (about ¼ onion)
1 garlic clove, minced (about ½ teaspoon)
455g ground beef (93% lean)
60g whole-wheat bread crumbs
60g crumbled feta cheese
1 large egg
½ teaspoon dried oregano, crushed between your fingers
¼ teaspoon freshly ground black pepper
125g 2% plain Greek yoghurt
40g chopped and pitted Kalamata olives
2 tablespoons olive brine
Romaine lettuce or pita bread for serving (optional)

Preparation:

1. Coat two 6-cup muffin pans with nonstick cooking spray and set aside. 2. In a small skillet, heat the oil over medium heat. Add the onion and cook for 4 minutes, stirring frequently. Add the garlic and cook for 1 more minute, stirring frequently. Remove from the heat. 3. In a large mixing bowl, combine the garlic, onion, ground beef, egg, oregano, bread crumbs, feta, and pepper. Gently mix them together with your hands. 4. Divide into 12 portions and place in the muffin cups. Working in batches, place the pan into the air fryer and cook at 200°C for 18 to 20 minutes, or until the internal temperature of the meat is 70°C on a meat thermometer. 5. While the meatloaves are baking, in a small bowl, stir together the yoghurt, olives, and olive brine. 6. When you're ready to serve, place the meatloaves on a serving platter and spoon the olive-yoghurt sauce on top. You can also serve them on a bed of lettuce or with cut-up pieces of pita bread.

Per Serving: Calories 231; Fat 11.79g; Sodium 329mg; Carbs 10.28g; Fibre 1.1g; Sugar 2.76g; Protein 21.29g

Chapter 7 Red Meat Mains | 59

Authentic Greek Moussaka

⏰ Prep: 25 minutes   🍲 Cook: 40 minutes   ❖ Serves: 6-8

Ingredients:

For the Aubergine:
910g aubergine, cut into ¼-inch-thick slices
1 teaspoon salt
2 to 3 tablespoons extra-virgin olive oil
For the Filling:
1 tablespoon extra-virgin olive oil
2 shallots, diced
1 tablespoon dried, minced garlic
455g ground lamb
115g portobello mushrooms, diced
1 (410g) can of crushed tomatoes, drained
25g tomato paste
240ml low-sodium beef broth
2 bay leaves
2 teaspoons dried oregano
¾ teaspoon salt
210g store-bought béchamel sauce
20g panko bread crumbs

Preparation:

To make the aubergine: 1. Line the baking sheets with paper towels and place the aubergine slices in a single layer, and sprinkle with salt. Place another layer of paper towels on the aubergine slices. Continue until all aubergine slices are covered. 2. Let the aubergine sweat for 30 minutes to remove excess moisture. While this is happening, make the meat sauce. 3. Pat the aubergine dry. Brush the air fryer basket with oil. 4. Working in batches, place the aubergine slices in the basket and cook at 230°C for 15 to 20 minutes or until lightly browned and softened. 5. Remove from the air fryer and cool slightly before assembling the moussaka.
To make the filling: 1. In a large, oven-safe sauté pan or skillet, heat the olive oil over high heat. Cook the shallots and garlic for 2 minutes, until starting to soften. 2. Add the ground lamb and brown it with the garlic and onions, breaking it up as it cooks. Add the mushrooms and cook for 5 to 7 minutes, or until they have dehydrated slightly. 3. Add the tomatoes and paste, bay leaves, oregano, beef broth, and salt and stir to combine. Once the sauce is simmering, lower to medium-low and cook for 15 minutes, or until it reduces to a thick sauce. Remove the sauce to a separate bowl before assembly. 4. Place half the aubergine slices in the bottom of the skillet used to make the sauce. Top the slices with all the meat filling. 5. Place the remaining aubergine on top of the meat filling and pour the jarred béchamel sauce over the aubergine. Sprinkle with the bread crumbs. 6. Place the pan into the air fryer and bake at 175°C for 30 to 40 minutes or until golden brown. 7. Let stand for 10 minutes before serving.
Per Serving: Calories 489; Fat 26.6g; Sodium 1572mg; Carbs 47.77g; Fibre 11g; Sugar 15.42g; Protein 21.81g

Homemade Greek Meatballs (Keftedes)

⏰ Prep: 20 minutes   🍲 Cook: 25 minutes   ❖ Serves: 4

Ingredients:

2 whole-wheat bread slices
570g ground turkey
1 egg
30g seasoned whole-wheat bread crumbs
3 garlic cloves, minced
¼ red onion, grated
15g chopped fresh Italian parsley leaves
2 tablespoons chopped fresh mint leaves
2 tablespoons chopped fresh oregano leaves
½ teaspoon sea salt
¼ teaspoon freshly ground black pepper

Preparation:

1. Line the air fryer basket with parchment paper or aluminum foil. 2. Run the bread under water to wet it, and squeeze out any excess. Tear the wet bread into small pieces and place it in a medium bowl. 3. Add the turkey, egg, red onion, parsley, mint, oregano, sea salt, bread crumbs, garlic, and pepper. Mix well. Form the mixture into ¼-cup-size balls. Place the meatballs in the prepared basket. 4. Cook at 175°C for about 25 minutes, or until the internal temperature reaches 75°C.
Per Serving: Calories 302; Fat 12.91g; Sodium 514mg; Carbs 13.93g; Fibre 1.9g; Sugar 1.55g; Protein 32.56g

Chapter 8 Sweets and Desserts

Poached Pears in Red Wine Sauce 62

Raspberry Meringues 62

Cinnamon Baked Apples with Walnuts 63

Chocolate Molten Lava Cake 63

Crispy Baklava with Walnuts 64

Pistachio Butter Cookies 64

Classic Crème Caramel 65

Crispy Cinnamon Sugar Biscotti 65

Semolina and Syrup Cake 66

French Cherry Clafoutis 66

Poached Pears in Red Wine Sauce

⏰ **Prep: 15 minutes**   🍲 **Cook: 60 minutes**   🍽 **Serves: 4**

Ingredients:

4 just-ripe firm pears, such as Bosc or Anjou
240ml sweet red wine, such as port or Beaujolais Nouveau
1 cinnamon stick
2 teaspoons light brown sugar
½ teaspoon pure almond extract
4 mint sprigs for garnish

Preparation:

1. Peel the pears, leaving the core and stem intact. Cut a slice from the bottom of each to allow them to stand easily. Place the pears in a small baking dish. 2. In a small saucepan, combine the red wine, cinnamon stick, and brown sugar and heat over low heat just until it reaches a simmer. Stir in the almond extract, remove the cinnamon stick, and pour the liquid into the baking dish. Slide the dish into the air fryer, being careful not to tip the pears. 3. Bake at 160°C until the pears are golden and fork-tender, about 1 hour. The bottom one-third to one-half will be a deep red. 4. Gently transfer the pears to a platter and pour the red wine mixture back into the saucepan. Heat over medium heat and simmer until reduced by half, about 15 minutes. Remove the pan from the heat and let the sauce cool for 10 minutes. 5. To serve, place each pear in a shallow dessert bowl and pour a little red wine sauce around it. Garnish with fresh mint.
Per Serving: Calories 127; Fat 0.56g; Sodium 7mg; Carbs 30.18g; Fibre 5.9g; Sugar 19.63g; Protein 0.82g

Raspberry Meringues

⏰ **Prep: 15 minutes**   🍲 **Cook: 50 minutes**   🍽 **Serves: 4**

Ingredients:

4 large egg whites, at room temperature
¼ teaspoon cream of tartar
Pinch sea salt
170g honey
120g raspberries

Preparation:

1. Line the air fryer basket with parchment paper and set aside. 2. In a large stainless steel bowl, beat the egg whites until they are frothy. 3. Beat in the cream of tartar and salt until soft peaks form, 4 to 5 minutes. 4. Beat in the honey, 1 tablespoon at a time, until stiff glossy peaks form. 5. Spoon the meringue batter onto the baking sheets by tablespoons and create a small well in the centre of each with the back of a spoon. 6. Working in batches if necessary, place the meringues in the air fryer basket and bake at 95°C until firm, 45 to 50 minutes. Turn off the heat in the air fryer and open to cool the meringues in the air fryer for at least 1 hour. 7. Store in an airtight container for up to 1 week and serve with a raspberry in the centre of each meringue. You can serve with other fruits if desired.
Per Serving: Calories 162; Fat 0.26g; Sodium 202mg; Carbs 38.95g; Fibre 2.1g; Sugar 36.39g; Protein 4.09g

Cinnamon Baked Apples with Walnuts

⏱ **Prep: 15 minutes**   🍲 **Cook: 45 minutes**   ❖ **Serves: 4**

Ingredients:

4 apples
30g chopped walnuts
2 tablespoons honey
1 teaspoon ground cinnamon
¼ teaspoon ground nutmeg
¼ teaspoon ground ginger
Pinch sea salt

Preparation:

1. Cut the tops off the apples and use a metal spoon or paring knife to remove the cores, leaving the bottoms of the apples intact. 2. In a small bowl, stir together the walnuts, nutmeg, ginger, honey, cinnamon, and sea salt. Spoon the mixture into the centres of the apples. 3. Place the apples cut-side up in the air fryer basket and bake at 190°C for about 45 minutes until browned, soft, and fragrant. 4. When done, serve warm.

Per Serving: Calories 162; Fat 3.64g; Sodium 148mg; Carbs 35.16g; Fibre 5.1g; Sugar 27.69g; Protein 1.31g

Chocolate Molten Lava Cake

⏱ **Prep: 5 minutes**   🍲 **Cook: 10 minutes**   ❖ **Serves: 4**

Ingredients:

Olive oil cooking spray
30g whole wheat flour
1 tablespoon unsweetened dark chocolate cocoa powder
⅛ teaspoon salt
½ teaspoon baking powder
85g raw honey
1 egg
2 tablespoons olive oil

Preparation:

1. Lightly coat the insides of four ramekins with olive oil cooking spray. 2. In a medium bowl, combine the flour, honey, egg, cocoa powder, salt, baking powder, and olive oil. 3. Divide the batter evenly among the ramekins. 4. Place the filled ramekins inside the air fryer basket and bake at 195°C for 10 minutes. 5. Remove the lava cakes from the air fryer and slide a knife around the outside edge of each cake. Turn each ramekin upside down on a saucer and serve.

Per Serving: Calories 178; Fat 8.12g; Sodium 99mg; Carbs 25.75g; Fibre 1g; Sugar 19.76g; Protein 2.54g

Crispy Baklava with Walnuts

⏱ **Prep: 10 minutes**　　🍳 **Cook: 40 minutes**　　📚 **Serves: 8**

Ingredients:

180g finely chopped walnuts
1 teaspoon ground cinnamon
¼ teaspoon ground cardamom (optional)
240ml water
100g sugar
170g honey
2 tablespoons freshly squeezed lemon juice
230g salted butter, melted
20 large sheets phyllo pastry dough, at room temperature

Preparation:

1. In a small bowl, gently mix the walnuts, cinnamon, and cardamom (if using) and set aside. 2. In a small pot, bring the water, honey, sugar, and lemon juice just to a boil. Remove from the heat. 3. Put the butter in a small bowl. On an ungreased baking pan, put 1 layer of phyllo dough and slowly brush with butter. Be careful not to tear the phyllo sheets as you butter them. Carefully layer 1 or 2 more phyllo sheets, brushing each with butter in the baking pan, and then layer ⅛ of the nut mix; layer 2 sheets and add another ⅛ of the nut mix; repeat with 2 sheets and nuts until you run out of nuts and dough, topping with the remaining phyllo dough sheets. 4. Slice 4 lines into the baklava lengthwise and make another 4 or 5 slices diagonally across the pan. 5. Put the baking pan in the air fryer and cook at 175°C for 30 to 40 minutes, or until golden brown. 6. Remove the baklava from the air fryer and immediately cover it with the syrup.

Per Serving: Calories 446; Fat 27.96g; Sodium 356mg; Carbs 51.31g; Fibre 2.2g; Sugar 24.1g; Protein 5.91g

Pistachio Butter Cookies

⏱ **Prep: 20 minutes**　　🍳 **Cook: 15 minutes**　　📚 **Serves: 6**

Ingredients:

125g all-purpose flour, plus extra for dusting
30g cornstarch
1 teaspoon baking powder
Pinch sea salt
1 large egg
60g confectioners' sugar
115g (1 stick) unsalted butter, at room temperature
½ teaspoon lemon zest
½ teaspoon pure vanilla extract
30g finely ground pistachios

Preparation:

1. Line the air fryer basket with parchment paper. 2. In a large bowl, stir the flour, cornstarch, baking powder, and salt until well blended. 3. Add the egg, butter, lemon zest, confectioners' sugar, and vanilla and stir until the dough is uniform. 4. Turn the dough out onto a lightly floured surface and flatten it out with your hands. Place the ground pistachios in the centre of the dough and knead the dough to evenly incorporate the nuts. 5. Roll the dough into 2-inch balls and place them on the prepared basket, then use your palm to flatten them slightly. 6. Bake at 200°C for 10 to 12 minutes, until golden brown. 7. Remove the cookies from the air fryer and let them cool before serving or storing.

Per Serving: Calories 293; Fat 15.94g; Sodium 214mg; Carbs 32.42g; Fibre 1.7g; Sugar 9.08g; Protein 5.91g

Chapter 8 Sweets and Desserts

Classic Crème Caramel

⏰ Prep: 20 minutes   🍳 Cook: 60 minutes   🍽 Serves: 6

Ingredients:

300g sugar, divided
120ml water, plus more as needed
710ml milk
4 large egg yolks
2 teaspoons vanilla extract
Grated zest of 1 orange

Preparation:

1. In a heavy-bottomed saucepan over low heat, add 200g of sugar and the water. Cook until the sugar dissolves, carefully brushing the walls of the pot with a little water to prevent the sugar from crystallising on the sides. 2. Increase the heat to medium-high and boil until a syrup forms and turns golden brown. Remove from the heat and carefully pour the syrup into 6 ramekins. Set aside to cool. 3. In a medium saucepan over medium heat, heat the milk until hot but not boiling. 4. In a medium bowl, whisk the egg yolks with the vanilla, the remaining 100g of sugar, and orange zest. While whisking continually, slowly add the warmed milk to the egg mixture, whisking until well combined. 5. Using a fine-mesh sieve, strain the milk-and-egg mixture into a bowl. Pour the strained mixture into the ramekins. Place the ramekins in a baking pan and add enough water to come halfway up the sides of the ramekins. 6. Put the baking pan in the air fryer and bake at 160°C for about 35 minutes or until the custard is just set. Remove from the air fryer, carefully remove the ramekins from the hot water, and let cool for 15 minutes. 7. Cover and refrigerate for 3 hours before serving. To unmold, run a sharp knife around the inside of each ramekin and carefully invert it onto a serving plate.
Per Serving: Calories 213; Fat 7g; Sodium 59mg; Carbs 31.61g; Fibre 0.1g; Sugar 30.85g; Protein 5.66g

Crispy Cinnamon Sugar Biscotti

⏰ Prep: 20 minutes   🍳 Cook: 55 minutes   🍽 Serves: 5

Ingredients:

250g all-purpose flour
3 teaspoons ground cinnamon, divided
1 teaspoon baking powder
¼ teaspoon salt
200g sugar, divided
6 tablespoons unsalted butter, at room temperature
3 large eggs
60ml freshly squeezed orange juice
1 teaspoon vanilla extract

Preparation:

1. Line the air fryer basket with parchment paper. 2. In a medium bowl, whisk 2 teaspoons of cinnamon, the flour, baking powder, and salt. Set aside. 3. In a large bowl, combine all but 2 tablespoons of sugar and the butter. Beat until fluffy with a handheld electric mixer. 4. Add 2 eggs and beat well to combine. Mix in the orange juice and vanilla until blended. 5. Add the flour mixture to the butter mixture and combine until a dough forms. Divide the dough in half. Shape each half into a 9-inch-long log or the size that fits your air fryer. 6. In a small bowl, whisk the remaining egg. Brush the logs with the egg wash. 7. Place the logs into the air fryer basket and bake at 160°C for 40 minutes. Remove and let cool for 20 minutes. Leave the air fryer on. 8. In a small bowl, stir together the reserved 2 tablespoons of sugar and the remaining 1 teaspoon of cinnamon. 9. Cut the logs at a 45-degree angle into ½-inch-thick slices with a serrated knife. Place the biscotti, cut-side down, on a baking sheet. Dust with the cinnamon-sugar and continue to bake for 15 minutes. Let cool for a couple of hours before serving.
Per Serving: Calories 400; Fat 12.64g; Sodium 168mg; Carbs 61.6g; Fibre 2.2g; Sugar 20.98g; Protein 9.64g

Semolina and Syrup Cake

⏱ **Prep: 15 minutes**　　🍳 **Cook: 40 minutes**　　🍽 **Serves: 12**

Ingredients:

1 tablespoon tahini
505g semolina flour, or uncooked Cream of Wheat cereal
155g Ghee, or store-bought, at room temperature
100g sugar
245g Plain yoghurt plus 1 tablespoon, or store-bought
1½ teaspoons baking soda
12 almonds
470g Orange Blossom Syrup

Preparation:

1. Coat a baking dish with the tahini. 2. In a medium bowl, stir together the ghee, semolina, and sugar. Set aside. 3. In a small bowl, whisk 245g of yoghurt with the baking soda. Set aside for 5 minutes. 4. Add the yoghurt mixture to the semolina mixture and mix well to combine. Pour the batter into the prepared baking dish. 5. Moisten your palms with the remaining 1 tablespoon of yoghurt and smooth the top of the cake. Lightly shake the pan to settle the batter. Lightly press a knife blade into the batter–do not cut all the way through— to mark 2-inch squares or diamond-shaped pieces. Place 1 almond in the centre of each piece. 6. Place the baking dish into the air fryer and bake at 200°C for 40 minutes or until golden. 7. Pour the syrup over the warm cake and let it soak into the cake. Let cool for at least 2 hours before serving.

Per Serving: Calories 215; Fat 2.43g; Sodium 170mg; Carbs 41.06g; Fibre 2.1g; Sugar 8.53g; Protein 6.8g

French Cherry Clafoutis

⏱ **Prep: 10 minutes**　　🍳 **Cook: 30 minutes**　　🍽 **Serves: 4**

Ingredients:

3 tablespoons melted butter, at room temperature, plus more for preparing the pan
65g all-purpose flour
100g sugar
¼ teaspoon salt
3 large eggs
Grated zest of 2 lemons
235ml whole milk
535g cherries, pitted
1 tablespoon powdered sugar, for serving

Preparation:

1. Coat a baking pan or other pan that fits your air fryer with butter. Set aside. 2. In a medium bowl, stir together the flour, sugar, and salt. Set aside. 3. In another medium bowl, whisk the eggs. Add the lemon zest, melted butter, and milk. Whisk to combine. Add the egg mixture over the flour mixture and whisk for about 3 minutes until very smooth. 4. Pour the batter into the prepared pan. Arrange the cherries on top. 5. Place the baking pan into the air fryer and bake at 175°C for 30 minutes or until the clafoutis is set and golden. Let cool for 10 minutes, and dust with the powdered sugar before serving.

Per Serving: Calories 271; Fat 13.05g; Sodium 277mg; Carbs 31.91g; Fibre 0.6g; Sugar 18.35g; Protein 7.16g

| Chapter 8 Sweets and Desserts

Conclusion

The Breville Smart Oven Air Fryer Pro cookbook serves as a culinary companion, unlocking the full potential of this versatile kitchen appliance. With a diverse array of recipes spanning appetizers, mains, sides, and desserts, it caters to every palate and occasion. From crispy golden fries to succulent roasted meats, each dish is crafted with precision and innovation, showcasing the appliance's multifunctionality. With detailed instructions and insightful tips, even novice cooks can effortlessly create restaurant-quality meals. Whether you're cooking for a family dinner or entertaining guests, the cookbook empowers you to elevate your cooking game and embrace the art of home cooking with confidence and flair.

Appendix Recipes Index

A
Air Fried Crab Cakes 32
Air Fried Turkey Meatballs 53
Air Fryer Ramekin Eggs 17
Authentic Greek Moussaka 60
Avocado Toast with Poached Eggs 18

C
Chard and Feta Frittata 18
Cheesy Spinach and Egg Pie 16
Chicken Artichoke Pizza with Olives 39
Chicken Kebabs with Tzatziki Sauce 54
Chinese Five-Spice Flavoured Popcorn 33
Chocolate Molten Lava Cake 63
Cinnamon Baked Apples with Walnuts 63
Classic Chicken Kebab with Vegetables 53
Classic Crème Caramel 65
Crispy Artichoke Hearts 26
Crispy Aubergine Slices 28
Crispy Baklava with Walnuts 64
Crispy Breaded Turkey Cutlets 50
Crispy Chicken Tenders 50
Crispy Cinnamon Sugar Biscotti 65
Crispy Honey Nut Granola 17
Crispy Pita Wedges 34
Crispy Polenta Fish Sticks 45
Crunchy Turmeric Roasted Chickpeas 33

D
Delicious Pollock Fillets with Roasted Tomatoes 47

E
Easy Air Fryer Popcorn 31
Easy Harissa Shakshuka 15

F
Flavourful Lasagna with Three Sauces 41
Fluffy Cheese Pancake 21
Foil Baked Fish with Garlic 46
French Cherry Clafoutis 66

G
Garlic Shrimp and Mushroom Pasta 46
Goat Cheese Crostini with Basil 32
Greek Beef Meatloaf 56
Greek Yoghurt Cornbread 40
Greek Yoghurt Deviled Eggs 31

H
Healthy Greek Yoghurt Parfait with Granola 20
Healthy Trail Mix 36
Herb Roasted Whole Chicken 51
Herbed Dijon Roasted Pork Tenderloin 59
Homemade Greek Meatballs (Keftedes) 60
Homemade Olive Tapenade Flatbread 21
Honey Glazed Carrots with Walnuts 24
Honey Glazed Salmon Fillets 48

K
Keto Courgette Muffins 15

L
Lamb Pita Pizza with Pine Nuts 40
Lemon Cauliflower with Saffron Dipping Sauce 36
Lemon Garlic Chicken Thighs 54
Lemon Tofu with Sun-Dried Tomatoes and Artichokes 27

M
Mashed Fava Beans Crostini 35
Mediterranean Chicken Thighs 52
Mini Carrot Bran Muffins 20
Mini Greek Meatloaves 59
Mixed Berry Baked Oatmeal 19

N
No-Knead Sesame Bread 42

P
Parmesan and Thyme Roasted Butternut Squash 28
Perfect Mediterranean Veggie Pizza 38
Pesto Pita Pizza with Mushrooms 38
Pistachio Butter Cookies 64
Poached Pears in Red Wine Sauce 62
Pork Roast with Apple Dijon Sauce 58
Provencal Salmon Fillets 44

R
Ramekin Baked Eggs with Swiss Chard, Feta, and Basil 19
Raspberry Meringues 62
Roasted Asparagus Caprese Pasta 41
Roasted Beef Tips with Yellow Onions 56
Roasted Beets with Fresh Dill 29
Roasted Broccoli Florets with Orange 29
Roasted Brussels Sprouts Salad with Almonds 25
Roasted Cauliflower Steaks with Baba Ghanoush 24
Roasted Fish Fillets with Green Beans and Tomatoes 47
Roasted Grape Tomatoes and Asparagus 26
Roasted Halibut in Parchment with Courgette and Thyme 48
Roasted Mini Potatoes 34
Roasted Pork Tenderloin and Lemony Orzo 57
Roasted Tomato, Aubergine, and Chickpeas 27
Roasted Vegetable Mélange 23
Rosemary Roasted Chicken Drumsticks 52

S
Salmon with Orange and Dill 45
Semolina and Syrup Cake 66
Simple Lamb Meatballs 57
Sriracha Lamb Chops 58
Star Anise-Glazed Carrots 25
Steamed Cod with Onions & Swiss Chard 44
Sumac Roasted Chicken with Cauliflower and Carrots 51
Sweet Anise Bread 42
Sweet Potato Toast with Vegetables and Eggs 16

T
Tabbouleh Stuffed Tomatoes0 23
Tasty Moroccan Courgette Spread 35

W
White Clam Pizza Pie 39

Printed in Great Britain
by Amazon